Personalities in
LOVE

OTHER BOOKS BY DONNA PARTOW

BECOMING A VESSEL GOD CAN USE

BECOMING THE WOMAN GOD WANTS ME TO BE:
A 90-DAY GUIDE TO LIVING THE PROVERBS 31 LIFE

BECOMING THE WOMAN I WANT TO BE:
A 90-DAY JOURNEY TO RENEWING SPIRIT, SOUL & BODY

THIS ISN'T THE LIFE I SIGNED UP FOR . . .
BUT I'M FINDING HOPE & HEALING

Personalities in

LOVE

UNDERSTANDING YOURSELF
AND THE MAN IN YOUR LIFE

DONNA PARTOW

Revell

a division of Baker Publishing Group
Grand Rapids, Michigan

Published by Revell
a division of Baker Publishing Group
P.O. Box 6287, Grand Rapids, MI 49516-6287
www.revellbooks.com

Originally published by Bethany House in 1998 under the title *A Woman's Guide to the Temperaments*

Printed in the United States of America

Library of Congress Cataloging-in-Publication Data
Partow, Donna.
    Personalities in love : understanding yourself and the man in your life /
Donna Partow.
        p.   cm.
    Rev. ed. of: A woman's guide to personality types.
    Includes bibliographical references (p.   ).
    ISBN 978-0-8007-3441-1 (pbk.)
    1. Christian women—Religious life. 2. Four temperaments. 3. Man-woman relationships—Religious aspects—Christianity. I. Partow, Donna. Woman's guide to personality types. II. Title.
BV4527.P379 2011
248.8'43—dc23   2011020680

Some names and personal details have been changed to protect the identity of those whose stories appear in this book.

11   12   13   14   15   16   17   7   6   5   4   3   2   1

This book is dedicated to two of the
"CLASS"iest women I know.

Florence Littauer
for being a living example of all I hope to be someday.
Thanks for daring me to dream.

and

Marita Littauer
who has so generously shared her time
and talents to equip me to pursue that dream.
Thanks for being a mentor and a friend.

CONTENTS

Contents

Foreword to the Original Edition

During the past thirty years, I've had the privilege of teaching the four personality types to audiences around the world. I've witnessed life-changing results in the hearts of anyone—doctors, pastors, laypeople—willing to apply these truths to their daily lives. Nowhere have these results been more profound or of more eternal significance than in the home. That's why I believe this book is so important. Donna Partow's book is the first one ever to apply the up-to-date findings of personality research to helping women maximize their roles as mothers, wives, and individuals.

In her unique, down-to-earth style, Donna has written a book that's light and breezy to read, while delivering a powerful message about the importance of the Bible's injunction to live with one another in an understanding way.

It's the kind of book a busy mom can pick up on the run, read a few pages, and walk away with something valuable—a new truth or fresh insight that will make an immediate difference in the way she approaches family life.

I have been acquainted with Donna's ministry for several years and have enjoyed sharing the platform with her at various Christian women's conferences. Donna is one of my Certified Personality Trainers and a graduate of CLASS, my speakers' training program. As such, I am delighted to commend to you both Donna and this book.

Florence Littauer
author, *Personality Plus*

Part One

UNDERSTAND YOURSELF

---------- I ----------

PERSONALITIES 101

Introduction

How's this for a bold opening statement: I believe this book can dramatically change your life for the better. I believe you now hold in your hands a set of tools no less tangible than the hammers hanging in your garage. Tools you can put to use—beginning today—to improve the quality of your relationship with your man and all those most important to you. It will even improve the quality of your interactions with neighbors, fellow churchgoers, store owners, waitresses, cashiers, and total strangers. Once you learn to quickly identify the personality of virtually everyone you meet, you'll discover just how handy this tool really is.

As I talk with women at conferences around the country, I'm continually amazed at how many of their deepest heartaches—especially in their romantic relationships and family life—are rooted in misunderstandings and personality conflicts. When I explain the Personality types, and especially the basic motivations and emotional needs of each, suddenly the lightbulbs go on. "Wow, if only I'd realized that's how he was wired!" or "So you mean he's not really trying to drive me nuts, that's just the way he is?" I wrote this book because I was determined to provide them—and you—with some practical solutions for relationship challenges.

Here's how *Personalities in Love* will help you:

- You'll gain an increased appreciation for the man in your life. Some of you may find that hard to believe, but I promise it's true! Even though opposites attract and then often attack, it doesn't have to be that way. Really, it doesn't! You don't have to battle with your husband for the rest of your married life or watch another dating relationship disintegrate when inevitable personality differences arise. I trust you'll find freedom in the realization that just because you disagree doesn't mean one of you is wrong and the other is right. You can conserve precious time and energy once you accept that you're simply looking at life through two very different lenses. And that's not only okay, it's a good thing.

- For those of you who are single, you will gain valuable insight into the Personalities of the men you date and how to communicate well despite your differences. You'll learn how your combined Personalities would likely affect a future marriage and which combinations tend to create the most peaceful and the most turbulent relationships. Armed with knowledge about the Personality types, you can make a wise choice about whom to marry, and how the two of you can work together to create wedded bliss.

- For those of you who have already said "I do," you'll learn the potential pitfalls in your marriage (based on the combined Personalities of you and your husband) and strategies to avoid them. You'll understand why some marriages are inclined to harmony, while others are more tempestuous by nature.

And as you read this book, I think you'll have a lot of fun along the way. When folks ask me what kind of writer I am, I always say, "I write for women in the bathroom."

Huh?

Yup, you read it right! I write for women in the bathroom, and if you know exactly what I'm talking about, then this book is definitely for you. I'm only able to read books about three pages at a time, in the stolen moments I manage to grab in the midst of my hectic life. I guess that brings us to another point: I always try to be honest about my less-than-perfect life. If you like writers who've got it all figured out, we could be in trouble from the get-go.

I haven't figured it all out, but I do know one thing: understanding the Personalities has been the single most helpful tool (after the Bible, of course) I've ever found for figuring out this crazy, mixed-up world and the fruits and nuts who populate it. It has even helped me make some sense of my own zany personality, and that's saying something.

Well, if none of those benefits sound worthwhile to you and you couldn't possibly profit by better understanding yourself and those around you, by all means, put this book down immediately! But if you suspect your relationship toolbox could use some new equipment, I encourage you to read on. But don't merely read; actively seek to put to use the things you are learning. The best way to do this is to:

- Read with a highlighter in your hand. Mark anything that makes you respond with a "Wow, *now* I get it." You can even mark the stuff that makes you shout, "My guy's got to read this!" (Not too many of those, though!)
- Take it a step further: jot down notes in the margins and at the end of each chapter, indicating how you can implement the information you've just learned.
- Share what you're learning with someone else or several someone elses! Why not start with your husband (or

boyfriend)? You can read him excerpts that strike you as particularly funny or enlightening. Better still, explain the concepts in your own words and try to think of your own stories to illustrate the Personalities in action. The best way to learn anything is to teach it to someone else.

- Enjoy the whole book, but focus on the emotional needs. Although I'm certainly happy you're reading my book, there won't be much point unless this material changes the way you relate to the people you love most. It won't be worth your time unless you invest the extra time required to apply the principles. Begin with the man of your life, actively trying to meet his emotional needs in fresh ways. See what a difference it makes in your marriage or dating relationship.

- Go back and reread the portions you highlighted. Copy some of the key points onto note cards and/or sticky notes, and review them on a regular basis.

- Continue reviewing the material on a routine basis, until it becomes part of the fabric of your life.

Some Background

You're probably familiar with the term *personality*, and maybe you have even attended a seminar where you charted your Personality type. The concepts I am presenting are far from new. In fact, they date back to the Greek physician and philosopher Hippocrates (460–377 BC), who first developed the theory. He identified four basic personalities: Sanguine, Melancholy, Choleric, and Phlegmatic. He attributed the differences to varying amounts of bodily substances: an abundance of blood caused a person to be Sanguine, black bile led to Choleric, yellow bile to Melancholy, and those with plenty of phlegm were Phlegmatic. We may chuckle at the theory, but it did have a biochemical basis, and in that sense it was definitely on target.

In 1966, Dr. Tim LaHaye, a pastor, author, and popular seminar speaker, took the Christian world by storm with his phenomenal bestseller *The Spirit-Controlled Temperament*. Florence Littauer picked up the baton in 1983, dedicating her own international best-seller, *Personality Plus*, to Dr. LaHaye. If you are a businessperson, perhaps you've been tested using the DISC Personality profile. It's exactly the same concept with different labels:

Dominant is the Choleric

Influencing is the Sanguine

Steady is the Phlegmatic

Conscientious is the Melancholy

What's unique about *Personalities in Love* is that it's written especially for women—wives, mothers, and single gals. And it's designed to help you where you live right now, in the midst of the daily juggling act: relationships with family and friends, career or ministry demands, cooking, cleaning, changing gazillions of diapers, flagging down school buses, or homeschooling. We're not going to waste any time on theory. That paragraph about Hippocrates was it, ladies! And you won't find any of the highfalutin' mumbo jumbo that some personality books are filled with. (You need a PhD just to read them!)

That's also why I won't be using the terms coined by Hippocrates. Instead, I'm going to refer to the Personalities based on the primary adjective that best describes each, as developed by Florence and Fred Littauer. The Sanguine's primary motivation in life is to have fun and be popular, so I'm calling her the Popular woman. Personally, I think it's just a whole lot easier to remember (not to mention *pronounce*) than the ancient *Sanguine*. The Choleric wants power and control, so she'll be easy to remember as the Powerful woman. The Melancholy is on a mission to bring perfection to an imperfect world, so I've dubbed her the Perfect woman. Last, but certainly not least, is the Phlegmatic type, whom Hippocrates claimed suffered from an overabundance of phlegm. As you'll soon discover, these women are so easygoing they probably wouldn't put up much of a fuss, but I sure wouldn't want to be associated with phlegm. Would you? Let's call her the Peaceful woman.

Okay, no ancient terminology and no psychobabble. What's left? Just practical help for your practical, everyday life. Like how to understand yourself—why you do what you do and why you find it so doggone hard to do the things you think you *ought to* and *want to* do. And how to understand others so you can get along better with your man and the other people around you.

Before we get to the really good stuff, I want to forewarn you about a couple of things. You may sense, at times, that I'm painting these Personality types in strictly primary colors. That's probably a fair assessment. First, it's because I'm a mom who spends lots of time around primary colors. But it's also because I think doing so makes these concepts easier to grasp. I do want to acknowledge, however, that even though I'm coloring with blue, red, and yellow, I know about that ninety-four-count Crayola box! We live in a world of many shades and nuances, but everything comes back to the primary colors. So, too, with the Personalities. Everyone you meet will be a unique blend, but the simplest way to understand a person is by understanding his or her underlying "colors."

For the same reason, you may notice that I've incorporated some rather extreme examples of the various Personality types in action. Again, I'm not saying that everyone with this Personality will always behave that way. Humans are notoriously unpredictable. Nevertheless, I think a glimpse at where the Personality weaknesses—left unchecked or pushed to an extreme—can lead a person is a powerful learning tool.

And one more thing! Please don't feel hopeless when you read about the weaknesses. Just as few people have all the strengths, few people have all the weaknesses. Even if you do recognize a particular weakness, you aren't doomed. These aren't intended as death sentences for your character. Rather than growing discouraged, pray that God will transform you from the inside out. You should also pray for the ones you love, that God will do a great work in their lives as well.

Therefore, if anyone is in Christ, he is a new creation; the old has gone, the new has come! All this is from God, who reconciled us to himself through Christ and gave us the ministry of reconciliation. (2 Cor. 5:17–18)

Without further ado, let's find out more about you. Any discussion of Personality must begin with understanding your own Personality type. Please take your time in working through the following Personality assessment tool, developed by Fred Littauer and used here with his kind permission.

Personality Profile[1]

Directions: In each of the following rows of four words across, place an X in front of the one word that most often applies to you. Continue through all forty lines. Be sure each number is marked. If you are not sure of which word *most* applies, ask a spouse or a friend, and think of what your answer would have been *when you were a child.* If you have questions about these descriptions, you'll find definitions of all terms in the appendix.

1. ☐ Adventurous	☐ Adaptable	☐ Animated	☐ Analytical
2. ☐ Persistent	☐ Playful	☐ Persuasive	☐ Peaceful
3. ☐ Submissive	☐ Self-sacrificing	☐ Sociable	☐ Strong-willed
4. ☐ Considerate	☐ Controlled	☐ Competitive	☐ Convincing

5.	☐ Refreshing	☐ Respectful	☐ Reserved	☐ Resourceful
6.	☐ Satisfied	☐ Sensitive	☐ Self-reliant	☐ Spirited
7.	☐ Planner	☐ Patient	☐ Positive	☐ Promoter
8.	☐ Sure	☐ Spontaneous	☐ Scheduled	☐ Shy
9.	☐ Orderly	☐ Obliging	☐ Outspoken	☐ Optimistic
10.	☐ Friendly	☐ Faithful	☐ Funny	☐ Forceful
11.	☐ Daring	☐ Delightful	☐ Diplomatic	☐ Detailed
12.	☐ Cheerful	☐ Consistent	☐ Cultured	☐ Confident
13.	☐ Idealistic	☐ Independent	☐ Inoffensive	☐ Inspiring
14.	☐ Demonstrative	☐ Decisive	☐ Dry humor	☐ Deep
15.	☐ Mediator	☐ Musical	☐ Mover	☐ Mixes easily
16.	☐ Thoughtful	☐ Tenacious	☐ Talker	☐ Tolerant
17.	☐ Listener	☐ Loyal	☐ Leader	☐ Lively
18.	☐ Contented	☐ Chief	☐ Chart maker	☐ Cute
19.	☐ Perfectionist	☐ Pleasant	☐ Productive	☐ Popular
20.	☐ Bouncy	☐ Bold	☐ Behaved	☐ Balanced
21.	☐ Blank	☐ Bashful	☐ Brassy	☐ Bossy
22.	☐ Undisciplined	☐ Unsympathetic	☐ Unenthusiastic	☐ Unforgiving
23.	☐ Reticent	☐ Resentful	☐ Resistant	☐ Repetitious
24.	☐ Fussy	☐ Fearful	☐ Forgetful	☐ Frank
25.	☐ Impatient	☐ Insecure	☐ Indecisive	☐ Interrupting
26.	☐ Unpopular	☐ Uninvolved	☐ Unpredictable	☐ Unaffectionate
27.	☐ Headstrong	☐ Haphazard	☐ Hard to please	☐ Hesitant
28.	☐ Plain	☐ Pessimistic	☐ Proud	☐ Permissive
29.	☐ Angers easily	☐ Aimless	☐ Argumentative	☐ Alienated
30.	☐ Naïve	☐ Negative attitude	☐ Nervy	☐ Nonchalant
31.	☐ Worrier	☐ Withdrawn	☐ Workaholic	☐ Wants Credit
32.	☐ Too sensitive	☐ Tactless	☐ Timid	☐ Talkative
33.	☐ Doubtful	☐ Disorganized	☐ Domineering	☐ Depressed
34.	☐ Inconsistent	☐ Introvert	☐ Intolerant	☐ Indifferent
35.	☐ Messy	☐ Moody	☐ Mumbles	☐ Manipulative
36.	☐ Slow	☐ Stubborn	☐ Show-off	☐ Skeptical
37.	☐ Loner	☐ Lords over others	☐ Lazy	☐ Loud
38.	☐ Sluggish	☐ Suspicious	☐ Short-tempered	☐ Scatterbrained
39.	☐ Revengeful	☐ Restless	☐ Reluctant	☐ Rash
40.	☐ Compromising	☐ Critical	☐ Crafty	☐ Changeable

Now you are ready to determine your Personality type. The following chart features the exact same word lists as the previous pages, but this time they are aligned underneath the appropriate Personality type. As you transfer your answers from your answer sheet to the following score sheet, you will see your Personality type revealed:

Personality Scoring Sheet

	Popular Sanguine	Powerful Choleric	Perfect Melancholy	Peaceful Phlegmatic
1.	☐ Animated	☐ Adventurous	☐ Analytical	☐ Adaptable
2.	☐ Playful	☐ Persuasive	☐ Persistent	☐ Peaceful
3.	☐ Sociable	☐ Strong-willed	☐ Self-sacrificing	☐ Submissive
4.	☐ Convincing	☐ Competitive	☐ Considerate	☐ Controlled
5.	☐ Refreshing	☐ Resourceful	☐ Respectful	☐ Reserved
6.	☐ Spirited	☐ Self-reliant	☐ Sensitive	☐ Satisfied
7.	☐ Promoter	☐ Positive	☐ Planner	☐ Patient
8.	☐ Spontaneous	☐ Sure	☐ Scheduled	☐ Shy
9.	☐ Optimistic	☐ Outspoken	☐ Orderly	☐ Obliging
10.	☐ Funny	☐ Forceful	☐ Faithful	☐ Friendly
11.	☐ Delightful	☐ Daring	☐ Detailed	☐ Diplomatic
12.	☐ Cheerful	☐ Confident	☐ Cultured	☐ Consistent
13.	☐ Inspiring	☐ Independent	☐ Idealistic	☐ Inoffensive
14.	☐ Demonstrative	☐ Decisive	☐ Deep	☐ Dry humor
15.	☐ Mixes easily	☐ Mover	☐ Musical	☐ Mediator
16.	☐ Talker	☐ Tenacious	☐ Thoughtful	☐ Tolerant
17.	☐ Lively	☐ Leader	☐ Loyal	☐ Listener
18.	☐ Cute	☐ Chief	☐ Chart maker	☐ Contented
19.	☐ Popular	☐ Productive	☐ Perfectionist	☐ Pleasant
20.	☐ Bouncy	☐ Bold	☐ Behaved	☐ Balanced
21.	☐ Brassy	☐ Bossy	☐ Bashful	☐ Blank
22.	☐ Undisciplined	☐ Unsympathetic	☐ Unforgiving	☐ Unenthusiastic
23.	☐ Repetitious	☐ Resistant	☐ Resentful	☐ Reticent
24.	☐ Forgetful	☐ Frank	☐ Fussy	☐ Fearful
25.	☐ Interrupting	☐ Impatient	☐ Insecure	☐ Indecisive
26.	☐ Unpredictable	☐ Unaffectionate	☐ Unpopular	☐ Uninvolved
27.	☐ Haphazard	☐ Headstrong	☐ Hard to please	☐ Hesitant

	Popular Sanguine	Powerful Choleric	Perfect Melancholy	Peaceful Phlegmatic
28.	☐ Permissive	☐ Proud	☐ Pessimistic	☐ Plain
29.	☐ Angers easily	☐ Argumentative	☐ Alienated	☐ Aimless
30.	☐ Naïve	☐ Nervy	☐ Negative attitude	☐ Nonchalant
31.	☐ Wants credit	☐ Workaholic	☐ Withdrawn	☐ Worrier
32.	☐ Talkative	☐ Tactless	☐ Too sensitive	☐ Timid
33.	☐ Disorganized	☐ Domineering	☐ Depressed	☐ Doubtful
34.	☐ Inconsistent	☐ Intolerant	☐ Introvert	☐ Indifferent
35.	☐ Messy	☐ Manipulative	☐ Moody	☐ Mumbles
36.	☐ Show-off	☐ Stubborn	☐ Skeptical	☐ Slow
37.	☐ Loud	☐ Lords over others	☐ Lone	☐ Lazy
38.	☐ Scatterbrained	☐ Short-tempered	☐ Suspicious	☐ Sluggish
39.	☐ Restless	☐ Rash	☐ Revengeful	☐ Reluctant
40.	☐ Changeable	☐ Crafty	☐ Critical	☐ Compromising

A Quick Introduction to Personalities

Now that you know which Personality type you are, I'll bet you're tempted to turn to the chapters about yourself first. That's okay. In fact, it's perfectly natural. But maybe you ought to stick around for a quick overview of all four Personality types before you dash off for further self-study. I promise it will be brief. Here's what we'll do. Let's pretend you've managed a short escape from your hectic life by enjoying lunch on a quiet bench in the local park. (Sounds nice, doesn't it?) While you're there, you meet each of the Personality types.

As you bite into your sandwich, you hear loud, uproarious laughter floating through the air. You notice a woman with long, flowing hair standing in the middle of a group. You also notice, even from a distance, that she's wearing a boldly colored outfit and great big dangly earrings. You couldn't *not notice* this woman if you tried. She demands attention. She is obviously talking a hundred miles a minute, and she's punctuating her delivery with wild, sweeping gestures. When you walk over to join the group, you realize this woman is not just talking, she's telling stories. If any story doesn't get the reaction she had hoped for, she immediately launches into a retelling of the *very same story*.

When she gets bored (you know, when anyone else starts talking), she dashes off and swings on the swings for a while, then strikes up a conversation with an old man on a nearby bench. For lunch, she breaks out a bag of McDonald's she picked up on the way to the park.

You've just met the *Popular* woman.

Although she's much quieter, you can't help noticing a strikingly attractive woman stylishly dressed in a freshly ironed outfit, complete with coordinating accessories. Her neatly manicured fingernails are tinted the same color as her lips. When you comment on her clothes, her face glows as she reports (in great detail) how she found them on the clearance rack of a fashionable store for 75 percent off. When she speaks, her voice is quiet and she uses very few gestures. In fact, she holds her arms close to her body. Her short, sleek hairstyle accentuates her facial features, which are carefully highlighted with just the right touch of makeup.

Throughout the afternoon, she keeps a careful watch over her perfectly dressed children. (Their outfits are ironed, too!) Her kids aren't allowed to play on the monkey bars, though, because she read an article in *Ladies Home Journal* that said monkey bars are the leading cause of playground accidents. When lunch rolls around, she unpacks nutritious sandwiches cut into perfect triangles, wrapped in plastic, then aluminum foil for extra safety.

You've just encountered the *Perfect* woman.

There's another woman sitting at a picnic table, working on what appears to be a very important project. Although she doesn't talk much, you get the feeling she's not shy, just preoccupied. From time to time, she gets up to organize an activity for the kids. Much to your surprise, she even disciplines *your* kids (with her hands on her hips and her pointing finger in their faces) for climbing an old apple tree. When she tells her own kids to come over for lunch, she speaks with authority, and the little tykes immediately come running. During lunch, she brings up the hot debate over the local school board referendum and lets everyone know just where she stands on the issue. It's not so much what she says as it is the authoritative tone in which she says it that lets you know this woman means business. Of course, the fact that she's carrying the latest-model electronic gadget will probably be your second clue!

You've witnessed the *Powerful* woman in action.

And finally, there's a very quiet woman who has laid out a picnic blanket. In fact, she has laid out two blankets, in case someone else needs a place to sit. She has brought along cold drinks and enough snacks to share with everyone. Although she doesn't talk about topics in great detail (and definitely doesn't venture an opinion during the discussion on the referendum), from time to time she'll speak up to offer food or drinks to the other women and children.

Speaking of children, you can't help noticing that her kids are almost always sitting on her lap. Even when they do venture off, she keeps them within eyesight. She may have brought along some of her older children, whom she homeschools. Although she and her kids are very sweet, you can't help noticing that their clothes are somewhat disheveled, and their grooming leaves something to be desired. When she sends one of her kids to retrieve something from their minivan, you notice it could use a trip to the car wash.

You've had an encounter with the *Peaceful* woman.

The Purse-onalities

When I speak at women's conferences, one of the most popular features is "The Purse-onalities." That's when I go out into the audience and dig through women's purses to illustrate their Personalities. Naturally, this exercise is an especially big hit with the women whose purse contents are *not* held up for all to see!

I'm convinced you really can tell a woman's Personality just by looking at her purse.

The Popular purse is huge, often more like a tote bag than a handbag. It might be cloth or plastic. Of course, you may spot a Popular woman carrying a cute little purse . . . but I guarantee there's a tote bag in the backseat of her car. They like fun purses with bright colors or animal prints. At a recent conference in California, one woman carried a huge, clear tote bag containing a cheetah print makeup case and a camera. The camera is not to take pictures of other people; it's so other people can take pictures of her. In another Popular purse, I found a package of multicolored, felt-tip markers and a key chain filled with self-descriptions like "diva" and "hotty." I pointed out that even if no one else told her how cute she was on any given day, her key chain did.

In contrast, the Perfect purse is small, top-quality leather, and features lots of compartments. The Perfect woman has a purse with a place for everything so she can keep everything in its place. I've seen Perfect purses that are smaller than the makeup case in most Popular women's purses. Just as she communicates on a need-to-know basis, she packs her purse on a need-to-have basis. And, of course, she cleans it out every night for what she describes as "obvious reasons."

The Powerful purse is often more like a briefcase. The Powerful woman's got all the latest electronics to help her juggle her many projects and boss her family around, even when she's not home! One woman in Florida had the ultimate Powerful purse: a soft leather attaché case with her company ID clipped on the outside and file folders bursting out the side. I'm sure some audience members think I "plant" these purses!

My favorite purse, however, belongs to the Peaceful woman. That's because it's more than a purse: it's a ministry tool. She sets out in the morning and goes forth into a hurting world, looking for those she can comfort. She has tissues in case anyone breaks down and cries. She carries enough medicine to qualify as a walking first-aid station. Throat lozenges for those with sore throats and aspirin for those with headaches. One woman carried Midol, even though she was in menopause by her own admission! Did you fall down? She's got Band-Aids *and* Neosporin. Of course, she always has plenty of hand sanitizer, because she knows if anyone gets sick, she's the one who'll play Florence Nightingale. Break a nail? No problem, she's got a file. Bad breath? She's got breath mints. Falling apart at the seams? She's got a sewing kit. I've been known to spend five minutes going through Peaceful purses. Sometimes I can't believe they pay me to have this much fun!

Typical Combinations

I hope the above descriptions gave you an idea of what each personality is like and maybe even a sense of how to spot them in a crowd. Naturally, it's a bit more complicated in real life because no two human beings are exactly alike. In addition, only 4 percent of the population is one Personality and one Personality only. The rest of us are a combination. Chances are, you've noticed that you are a combination of two Personalities. The most frequently occurring combinations include Popular-Powerful, Perfect-Peaceful, Powerful-Perfect, and Popular-Peaceful.

The following chart should help you visualize the most common combinations, because they always occur in side-by-side or top-and-bottom boxes and are never created by crossing boxes:

Popular	Powerful
Peaceful	Perfect

Unlikely Combinations

There are some combinations that should throw up a warning sign: combinations that do not occur naturally. Now don't panic, I'm not saying you are crazy or weird or anything like that. Just that you are letting outside forces shape who you are, rather than being the person you were originally created to be. You might think you're happy as a bug in a rug with your life, but maybe you'd be even happier (like a bug on a magic carpet ride) if you got back in touch with the real you.

Let me give you some examples of what I'm talking about. If your chart shows you are Popular-Perfect or Powerful-Peaceful, something may be fishy. Think about it. A person whose primary motivation in life is having fun (Popular woman) is not usually going to be concerned with doing everything perfectly (Perfect woman). And a person whose primary motivation is to take life easy (Peaceful woman) is not inclined to try to control everything around her (Powerful woman). These Personality types are polar opposites.

Just remember: typical combinations have aligning boxes; unlikely combinations "cross the line."

What does it mean if your score reveals contrasting Personalities? There are a few possibilities. Perhaps you had overpowering parents who forced you to become something you weren't. Or perhaps your birth order played a major role. For example: you were the firstborn and you had a Popular Personality, but your parents worked day and night to make you perfect, so you ended up demonstrating many Perfect traits. Conversely, you may have been born with a Perfect Personality, but your parents pushed you to become the cheerleader and the life of the party. You began playing the part of the Popular person, although it wasn't the real you. Or your husband is a pastor and even though you are a Powerful person with lots of drive, you feel the congregation expects you to stay quietly in the background. You're afraid they won't accept the real you, so you put on a false Peaceful mask.

The key for your self-understanding is getting back in touch with who you were as a child. Or simply look at who you are when you're at your very best, your most alive. That's the ultimate you. (If you discover contrasting Personalities, I encourage you to read

Your Personality Tree by Florence Littauer. It will help you work through these issues and get to know the real you.)

Now, what if you were a little bit of each Personality type? Well, that could mean one of three things.

Option #1: You are spiritually mature and well-balanced in all areas of life. You know how to kick back and have a great time, but you also know when to take life seriously. You know when it's appropriate to take charge of the situation, but you're not lacking in diplomacy. If you have walked in a close relationship with God for many years, you have simply become a reflection of your Teacher. Wonderful! The world would be a better place if there were more people like you.

Option #2: Perhaps you don't know yourself very well and you checked the wrong traits. Or you checked off what you thought you *should* be or *hope* to be, rather than what you really are. Have your spouse or a close friend take the test for you and see what the results are. Warning: you may not like the answers you get.

Option #3: You are an easygoing Peaceful type who didn't think the test was that big of a deal, so you just checked whatever came to mind. Again, invite your spouse or a friend to take the test on your behalf. If you really are the Peaceful type, you don't need to worry. They'll check off all nice stuff. After all, virtually everybody likes the easygoing Peaceful types.

Primary Motivations

In terms of understanding both yourself and the people around you, one of the most powerful tools at your disposal is understanding the underlying motivation behind each Personality's behavior. Understanding your own motivations will enable you to be more realistic. In other words, is it realistic to think life will always be fun or perfect or under control or easy? Of course not! Recognizing that will enable you to adjust your expectations and keep your frustration level to a minimum.

As you'll see in a moment, virtually everyone you meet is motivated by a desire for life to be either fun, perfect, under control, or easy. That's a bit simplistic, but as you work through this book—and evaluate whether or not the principles hold up in the real world—I think you'll discover that human motivations are often surprisingly simple. Once you understand their primary motivation, you can deal with people on their terms, which will make them far more inclined to respond favorably to you. Let's look at each Personality type in turn:

- The Popular type wants to have fun and be loved. When dealing with this type, ask yourself: "How can I make this more fun?"
- The Perfect type wants to bring perfection to an imperfect world, so ask yourself, "How can I do this in an orderly fashion?"
- The Powerful type wants to control as much of her world as possible, so ask yourself, "How can I give this person a sense of ownership in this situation?"
- The Peaceful type wants to take life easy and live in peace. To make the most of your relationship with him, ask yourself, "How can I promote harmony in this situation?"

We'll come back to these issues again and again throughout the book, providing you with a more careful look at how these motivations play out in your own heart and in relationship to the man of your life. For now, you've had your quick introduction to the four Personality types. You're ready to learn all you can about yourself and the people around you. Happy reading!

2

INTRODUCING THE POPULAR WOMAN

The first woman I'd like to introduce you to is the adorable, excitable Popular woman. She was a cheerleader in high school, and now she's the unofficial Cheerleader of Life! The Popular woman is probably the easiest Personality to spot in a crowd. She's the one talking a hundred miles a minute, laughing loudly, and waving her arms in the air. I say "crowd" because she's always in the middle of the action, mixing and mingling with people, regaling them with grand stories that may bear little or no resemblance to the truth.

Other Personality types watch her in action and think, *Doesn't she ever get tired?* They don't realize *this* is how she recharges her batteries. What a nice, relaxing bath does for other women, an *audience* does for the Popular woman. That's why she's the ultimate networker. By the way, if you're new in town or at the church, just link up with a Popular woman—she knows absolutely everyone. Soon, you'll have all kinds of vicarious friends.

Popular Strengths

I remember when Denise moved into the neighborhood. The first time we met, I thought, *This is magic. All my life I've dreamed of finding a friend like this. I know we will be best friends for life.* Little did I know that everyone who met Denise was thinking the very same thing. It's a tough assignment to be the whole world's best friend, but Denise does a pretty remarkable job of it.

You see, the Popular woman is everyone's very best friend, and she sincerely loves them all. However, she has an extra special place in her heart for friends who adore and idolize her—in other words, she thrives on compliments. However, if you don't make your worship obvious, she won't lose much sleep over it. In fact, even if you flat-out hurt her feelings, she won't hold a grudge. If she finds out she's done you wrong, she'll be quick to apologize. In fact, she's quick about just about everything. She's spontaneous and excitable. She's the kind of friend who calls you to say, "Let's go to the Bahamas . . . this weekend." And she's so persuasive, she just might talk you into it. No wonder she's everyone's very best friend!

Talkative

Generally speaking, the Popular woman is generally speaking. No doubt about it, she has what's commonly called the gift of gab. This woman makes a great teacher and speaker because she can talk twenty-four hours a day, on any topic, with or without information. She doesn't really even need a group; an audience of one will suffice. Groups are *preferred*, of course! You see, the Popular woman can talk to anyone, anywhere, anytime, about anything. Which is why her phone is permanently attached to her ear. She's a prime candidate to wear the T-shirt that says, "Help, I'm on the telephone and I can't shut up!"

If you try to call her, you'll never get through. Unless, of course, she has call-waiting. In which case, you can expect your phone conversation to be interrupted every few minutes by another of her 1,001 friends.

My friend Jill recently told me the following story.

Through my business, I had been talking with a woman from California for months, but we had never met in person. When I found out she was coming to Arizona, I invited her to join me for lunch. I'd never seen a picture of her, but I figured, *How many women will be waiting at Applebee's for a lunch partner? I'll find her, no problem.* Well, I got to the restaurant a few minutes late and asked if there were any women waiting for someone to join them. Sure enough, she was there first. I practically ran over to the table. She stuck out her hand to shake, and I said, "Oh, come on, let's hug" and gave her a huge hug. I sat down and started talking and talking. I did think some of the things she said were weird, like she thought I was in the manufacturing industry. But I found lots in common to talk about, so I didn't pay that much attention.

Then I asked her how the baby was doing. I thought she looked awfully old to have a baby, but I thought, *Hey, women are having babies later in life these days.* Anyway, this time she looked at me like I was nuts and said, "I only have one child and she's twenty-seven years old." Suddenly a light went on and I said, "May I see your business card?" I took one look and realized she was the *wrong* person. I cleared my throat and said, "Um, I don't know how to say this, but . . . I'm not your lunch date, and you're not mine. I wonder if they're eating lunch together!" I jumped up and ran to the front of the restaurant. Sure enough, my real lunch date was sitting there waiting.

Only the Popular type can talk to a total stranger for twenty minutes and not even realize she's talking to a total stranger!

Life of the Party

Her bright, cheery smile and bubbly personality make her the life of the party. And does she ever like to party! She likes to throw parties. She likes to attend parties. She loves to laugh and can have a great time doing just about anything. She's a one-woman party waiting to happen and usually arrives fashionably late singing the old Cindy Lauper tune, "Girls just wanna have fun!" Her primary goal is to enjoy life. If things get too serious, she's the first to try to lighten things up.

If your church or organization is planning a special event, put her in charge. I don't care if you're planning to sit around and watch the grass grow, she'll have everyone convinced it's the most happening event of the century. Even if she only turns out her inner circle of friends, you'll have about 250 people in attendance. She loves promoting and talking up future events. For her, the future is full of promise. That's because she always expects the best from people and from life. She's a whirlwind of action and energy. She can go-go-go for hours, weeks, and years on end.

Motivator

The Popular woman can motivate others to action. She's fabulous at dreaming up wild schemes that someone else can do. She has an uncanny ability to inspire normally sane people to do the wackiest things.

Sue's brother, John, is the most mild-mannered man you would ever meet. Unless, of course, you met Sue's husband first. Well, one St. Patrick's Day, when she was hosting another of her famous holiday festivals, she persuaded these two guys to install green toilet paper and green toilet fresheners, cover all the lamps (including the ceiling lamps, of course) with green napkins, and then practically wallpaper the neighborhood with green signs pointing to her house. These are gentlemen who would never call attention to themselves under ordinary circumstances, and here they were canvassing the neighborhood in outlandish costumes complete with sparkling green headgear.

Creative

She's a very creative dresser and likes to continually reinvent herself with new hairstyles and colors. She may not take the time to sew, but she sure is great at accessorizing with anything that sparkles. Her creativity extends beyond her personal appearance to everything she does: decorating, baking, entertaining. She'll throw together the most incredible Fourth of July cake and have everyone amazed. Don't ask her for the cake-making directions, though. Just as you've never seen a cake quite like that one before, you'll never see its likes again. Why? Because it never even occurred to her to write down the recipe. She'd rather come up with something brand-new the next time around.

When my friend Jill told me her four-and-a-half-year-old daughter, Jesse, plays quietly for hours in her bedroom each morning, I couldn't believe it. Then Jill told me about the room, and I *could* believe it. In fact, I wanted to rush over and play in the room myself! The headboard is a gigantic cutout cloud. The back wall is painted royal blue and has a big cutout moon and stars. That's the nighttime wall. Together, Jill and Jesse created a daytime wall by sponge-painting it light blue and white. Then her husband cut out and mounted wooden clouds. The window even has a cloud-shaped curtain.

All of the walls are covered with removable abstract stickers, so Jesse can redecorate her room any time she likes. She has a Japanese futon for her dolls, a large beanbag chair, and a shelf bursting with colorful picture books. Jill removed the door from the large closet and filled it with space organizers and shelf units that her husband bought at a local do-it-yourself store. (She put her Perfect husband in charge of that project!) One area is filled with building blocks, marble towers, and Tinkertoys. Another shelf holds board games.

There's an entire art center with lots of messy things to do. Wouldn't you spend hours in a room like that?

Accepting

The Popular woman lives by the maxim "Live and let live." Since her primary life goals are having fun and being loved by everyone, she doesn't waste time evaluating what's wrong with the people she meets. She'd rather focus on what's *right* about people and about life. She accepts the fact that everyone has faults, everyone makes mistakes. She has no desire to set herself up as judge and jury. And since no one likes to be judged, this characteristic goes a long way in promoting her personal popularity. This woman has many winsome qualities, but one of the most endearing is her childlike faith and trust in her fellow human beings. She always believes the best about others.

Although she likes to talk and may even engage in idle gossip, you'll rarely find her spreading vicious rumors. Even when someone deserves, by most standards, to be judged and censored, she'll resist the chorus of condemnation. Instead, she'll hold steadfastly to what is good in that person. More importantly, she willingly entrusts her life to the loving care of her heavenly Father. As a result, she is not plagued by worry and fear as people of other Personality types are. She takes each day as it comes, considering it a gift from God.

Popular Weaknesses

Too Talkative

The Popular woman often wonders why everyone else is so quiet all the time. She thinks to herself, *Oh, how tragic: a world filled with painfully shy people. Well, thank God I'm here to fill all that dead airtime with captivating stories and irresistible jokes.* But let me encourage you Popular women to conduct an experiment. See what happens if you keep quiet for more than five minutes.

(Unless you are the Popular type, you have no idea how difficult it will be to conduct this experiment!) No doubt you'll discover that, oddly enough, all those painfully shy people suddenly have plenty to say.

Her tendency to talk too much, combined with her lack of attention to details, often leaves the Popular woman with a case of the dreaded "foot-in-mouth" disease. Because she doesn't pay attention to little details such as whom she's talking to, what that person's name is, or what's appropriate, yet feels compelled to say something, she may say the wrong thing. In the process, she embarrasses herself, her family, and the people around her.

I remember attending a funeral where such an event unfolded. I watched as a bright, bubbly Popular woman marched over to the next of kin and burst out with all the enthusiasm she could muster: "I'm so excited to be here." Oops. She had no idea what to say, but that didn't stop her from speaking up.

Permissive

Let's imagine you stop by to see the Popular woman one afternoon. You're trying to have a conversation with her, and meanwhile, her kids are jumping up and down on the brand-new couch and coloring the walls with permanent markers. She doesn't even seem to notice. After all, discipline? What's that?

Her kids don't take her seriously, and she is permissive to the point that her kids become the terror of the neighborhood. She may wink and laugh and look the other way pretending not to notice, but if she doesn't rein in that little tribe soon, they might end up in serious trouble.

She's the eternal optimist, and usually that's great—it can enable her to handle the hassles of today, knowing brighter days are ahead. But pushed to extremes, her optimism becomes denial. She may ignore issues or danger signs in her marriage with a shrug of her shoulders, "Well, things will get better." Or she may overlook relationship warning signs during the dating phase. The Popular woman tends to avoid confrontation. Since her goal in life is to have fun, she puts off dealing with problems. She may have the time of her life planning a gala wedding with her Mr. Right, but if she refuses to acknowledge disagreements with her fiancé, she may be sabotaging her future marriage. Relationship conflicts are inevitable, but when the Popular woman ignores them rather than working through them with her man, she only allows the issues to fester and grow.

Forgetful

Thus far, I've resisted the temptation to confess my own sins. But this Popular woman trait hits so close to home, I just have to share a personal story. This was the year that we absolutely, positively wouldn't give in to the Halloween madness. *Well, we'll just have to come up with an alternative,* I thought. So when I received a flyer from a huge local church advertising a fall festival, I thought, *Aha! We'll go have a blast. Then when the kids start moaning and groaning on Halloween, I'll remind them what a great time we had bobbing for apples and carving pumpkins at the church festival.*

I woke up bright and early Saturday morning and began rallying the troops for the anticipated festival. How much better this would be than any dumb old trick-or-treat nonsense, I declared. Then the thought crossed my mind, *Gee, Donna, maybe you should double-check the time on that flyer.*

Now, of course, there was one small problem. And you fellow Popular women already know what it was. I had absolutely no clue where I had put that flyer. It had entered my mind when I first read the flyer that I should write the information down on my handy-dandy daily planner. But I think it pretty much goes without saying that, at the time, I had absolutely no clue where my handy-dandy-guaranteed-to-get-you-organized organizer was.

As my dressed-and-ready-to-go gang anxiously awaited our impending departure, I ransacked my home office. After fifteen minutes of ripping through piles of papers, I called out triumphantly, "Here it is." A few seconds elapsed, and I whispered sheepishly, "It was last night." It's funny on paper. But I can assure you, my heartbroken children weren't laughing.

By the way, when I noticed the date on the flyer, I realized I had also forgotten my niece's thirteenth birthday. I doubt she was laughing, either. Forgetfulness is a real weakness for the Popular woman.

Unreliable

The Popular woman is a big-picture person. She'll come up with a creative idea for a Christmas party and get all excited about the concept. Now, implementing the concept is a whole different story. Her battle cry is "Don't bore me with the details." She would never dream of doing things by the book. In fact, she can't be bothered to even open the book. Come to think of it, she probably couldn't even find the book!

This lack of attention to detail can get her into all kinds of minor mishaps and, sometimes, serious trouble. Little stuff like forgetting to put gas in the car can lead to big stuff like breaking down on the way to an important appointment. She makes commitments without thinking about what it will actually take to follow through, and as a result, she may leave a trail of broken promises behind. If she's not careful, she can inadvertently cause resentment in her closest relationships—all because she doesn't want to be bored with little things—like doing what she promised to do, when and how she promised to do it.

She loves to wing it, and sometimes she creates fabulously fun meals, funky clothes, and nifty art projects. But quite often, her cavalier attitude leads to a great big mess and a final product that's far from what she hoped and promised to deliver. In short, she's unreliable.

Fussy

If the Popular woman so much as loads the dishwasher, she's singing, "Nobody knows the trouble I've seen." She just can't seem to do a speck of work without fussin' and complainin'. She's driving to the grocery store a-fumin' and a-frettin' over traffic. Then she's a-grumblin' and a-groanin' about what's out of stock. She's shifting her weight from hip to hip, tossing disapproving glances at the checkout clerk who's taking too long. She's in a big hurry to get home (an hour ago she was in a big hurry to get *out* of the house, now she's in a hurry to get *back in* the house). Every once in a while she'll stop and hear herself, and maybe she'll even realize what people around her may be thinking: *You're not very much fun to be with right now!*

There's one simple reason why the Popular woman does so much fussing and fretting: she just plain doesn't like to work. Let's face it: work is no fun! *Volunteering* for work is fun, but following through and actually *doing* the work is another gig entirely.

Messy Housekeeper

Sometimes the Popular woman is so messy, she gets on her own nerves. She never seems to know where anything is! That's why leaving the house is such a huge ordeal for her. She loves *being* out of the house; it's *getting* out of the house that does her in.

First, she has to take a shower. That's a problem because she doesn't know where the fresh towels are. Then she has to style her hair, which is a hassle because she doesn't know where her curlers are. Where could she have left her makeup bag? Of course, she rarely has anything clean and ironed to wear, but more about that in a minute. I think it pretty much goes without saying that she doesn't know where her keys are, and where in the world did she set her purse when she came home last night?

We've said the Popular woman can have a great time doing just about anything. Well, actually, there is *one* thing she doesn't have a good time doing: cleaning the house. Her motto is, "If you came to see me, welcome. If you came to see my house, you're gonna need an appointment." I wish you could see my bathroom counter. Actually, I wish *I* could see my bathroom counter. I firmly believe it exists, but I haven't seen any evidence of it in lo, these many years. All my life, my living quarters have been a wreck. When I was a kid, my bedroom was always a wreck. I'll never forget the time when Larry, the boy of my elementary school dreams, came to spend the night with my brother, Danny. He was walking down the hallway, unbeknownst to me, when I made my fatal error: I opened my bedroom door. Well, if old Larry ever had any marriage intentions toward me, I could see by the look on his face that they had just evaporated.

My dorm room was a wreck. As I recall, the only way I could figure out which outfit I wanted to wear was by process of elimination. I'd try on each outfit in the closet, decide I didn't want to wear it, and throw it on the floor. By the time I hit upon the outfit I did want to wear for the day, it looked like it had been raining skirts and scarves. My dorm room was so bad, my roommate started a business selling tickets to view the spectacle: "Step right up, coeds. Come see for yourself. It's a miracle in progress: This girl lives like this and has not caught any communicable diseases."

My cleaning skills have not improved over the years! I got a call from my teenager one Saturday afternoon, cautiously inquiring into the current condition of the house. She had cleaned the whole house on Thursday. (Thank God she had misbehaved on Wednesday so I could dole out punishment in the form of chores.) Anyway, we'd managed to hold our ground on Friday so that when she left to spend the night at a friend's house around five o'clock, you could still see the floors. Now she wanted to bring her friend to our house and wanted to know if it was safe.

"Well, remember that lesson we had on hospitality the other night. You know, how you shouldn't be so concerned about having a perfect house. How people actually feel more comfortable when your house isn't perfect?"

"Yeah," she remembered.

"Well, I think you have an exciting opportunity to make your girlfriend *very* comfortable if you bring her on home right about now."

Overwhelming

As you can imagine from the previous illustrations, not everyone thinks the Popular woman is adorable. In fact, some folks just can't stand her. Their number-one objection? She's too *overwhelming!* The husband of one of my best friends refers to me only as "That Partow woman." This is no joke! I've only been in the man's presence on a few very brief occasions, but I guess even that was a bit too much.

Another Popular woman, Sandy, tells the story of her first experience volunteering at her church shortly after she became a Christian:

I was so excited about serving God and sharing the things I was learning. But since I was young and inexperienced, they [the church staff] told me the only assignment I was qualified for was working as an assistant in the five-year-olds' Sunday school class. Basically, I was in charge of supervising the cutting and pasting. It didn't matter to me, though. I loved having fun with the children. The teacher was a stern old woman who had been teaching for many, many years. In fact, her granddaughter was in the class. When the little girl arrived each Sunday morning, she always ran past her grandmother, straight over to my table. It was awkward, but there wasn't much I could do about it. I truly adored all the children and enthusiastically showered them with affection, while the older woman never displayed any emotion. I always got the feeling that this woman didn't like me very much.

Then one day, I received a four-page letter in the mail from my beloved colaborer in Christ, ripping me limb from limb. The final sentence (right before "Yours in Jesus' Name") was, "You are the most OVERWHELMING person I have ever met." I never stepped into that classroom again.

The Popular woman can indeed overwhelm people when her strengths are carried to extremes.

Seems Phony

Even when the Popular woman is at her best, people of other Personality types may misunderstand her motives. The following scenario reveals how the Popular woman can appear phony, even when her intentions are good.

Rhonda was an outgoing and active member of her church. One day, she received a call from her pastor. "Rhonda," he said, "you are such an encouragement to my wife. I have a special assignment for you. I met a young pastor's wife who is about your age, and she is struggling with depression. My wife and I thought perhaps you could attend her church on Sunday evenings and befriend her." She was thrilled with the assignment.

So off she went in hopes of cheering up the depressed pastor's wife. Rhonda recalls what happened.

I took one look around the church and thought, *Well, no wonder she's depressed. Everyone around here is so quiet.* So I started talking nonstop, trying to fill the void. That didn't quite solve it. Then I thought, *Oh, I know what the problem is. Everyone around here is so serious. Just thinking about it has got me depressed.* So I started cracking jokes. Well, she still seemed depressed, and I finally figured out why. *No wonder she's down in the dumps; this place is so cold!* So I began giving out hugs and double-cheek kisses to everyone who would stand still long enough.

Then I got a phone call. . . .

The woman I was supposed to be helping apparently did not find any of these activities helpful or amusing. I couldn't believe how angry she was at me, and I'll never forget her words: "You are the biggest phony I have ever met in my life. Every time I see you hug someone, it makes me want to puke. You claim to love people. If you really loved as Jesus loved, you would be *on time!*"

Rhonda didn't realize that the woman she was dealing with was the Perfect woman. And, as you will soon discover, the Perfect woman is the last person on earth who wants to be hugged and kissed and made a spectacle of. She places a high priority on promptness, following through on commitments, and doing things in the proper order, all of which were qualities that Rhonda admits she lacked. Looking back, Rhonda notes, "If only I had understood the Personality types back then, I could have been more sensitive to her needs. Now, when I deal with women who are the Perfect type, I make a special effort to be prompt, to deliberately speak more softly, and to respect their need for personal space."

What an illustration that story is of the clash of Personalities. God created one woman to dish out hugs and kisses just as he created the other to bring quiet beauty and order into the world. We need to be so careful before we cast judgment on another person. It could be that God created that person to touch lives in a way you never could. Remember, just because someone is different from you doesn't mean she's wrong. If you take away no other lesson from reading this book, I hope you'll take that one.

Making the Most of Your Personality Type

Your first step toward making the most of your Popular Personality is heeding the advice you've no doubt heard your whole life: talk less and listen more. It's corny, but true: God gave you two ears and one mouth. Try using them in that ratio. The Bible abounds with warnings about the dangers of the tongue. It says we're going to be held accountable for every word we speak. Can you imagine that? Some of us are going to stand there giving an account for a very long time.

Why not invest time reading and meditating on the book of James? It has much to say about the tongue, including this:

> When we put bits into the mouths of horses to make them obey us, we can turn the whole animal. Or take ships as an example. Although they are so large and are driven by strong winds, they are steered by a very small rudder wherever the pilot wants to go. Likewise the tongue is a small part of the body, but it makes great boasts. Consider what a great forest is set on fire by a small spark. The tongue also is a fire, a world of evil among the parts of the body. It corrupts the whole person, sets the whole course of his life on fire, and is itself set on fire by hell. All kinds of animals, birds, reptiles and creatures of the sea are being tamed and have been tamed by man, but no man can tame the tongue. It is a restless evil, full of deadly poison. (James 3:3–8)

Speaking of the tongue, you may also need to come to grips with the tendency to exaggerate. In reality, exaggeration is often nothing more than lying with a socially acceptable label attached. Suddenly it's not such a cute little sin. Suddenly it's on the list of the Ten Commandments. Is it possible that you have exaggerated some of your favorite stories so wildly for so long that you have actually started believing them yourself? A sobering experience might be to sit down and give an accurate account of what happened. You may realize how far the exaggeration game can take you from the truth.

Many Popular women tend to be self-centered and self-absorbed. Just as a small example, do you remember the names of new people you meet? Do you even listen for their names? Or do you figure, "Hey, they'll get to know me; that's all that matters"? As your heart condition improves, so will your ability to recall names. Wait and see!

Do you tend to forget everything? I have a terrible habit of jotting important information on slips of paper and promptly losing them. A woman recently left a message on my voice mail, saying she wanted to order twelve books (that's $120—money I could surely use). She said her name was Barb, indicated we had talked previously, and hung up. Now, I have no idea who Barb is or where I might have written her number. I spent an hour looking, but never found her phone number.

The most revolutionary change in my life came after reading *Disciplines of the Beautiful Woman*, which recommended carrying a personal notebook. I have been using one, to a greater or lesser extent, for the past thirty years. The trick is finding a daily planner that's big enough to hold everything you want to organize, yet small and convenient enough that you'll actually carry it with you wherever you go. If you don't carry it everywhere, it's really no use at all.

Another revolution occurred in my life when I recognized the importance of spending time with people who were a positive influence, even if it meant scheduling them into my life. No matter how hectic things get, I spend every Monday night with a group of godly women who challenge me to grow. Let me urge those of you who share this Personality type with me: be careful who you spend time with. Since you love approval, you tend to be more easily led astray than women with other Personality types. If you start hanging with the wrong group of women, they can definitely bring you down.

A great passage of the Bible for you to memorize is Psalm 1:

Blessed is the [woman] who does not walk in the counsel of the wicked or stand in the way of sinners or sit in the seat of mockers. But [her] delight is in the law of the LORD, and on his law [she] meditates day and night. [She] is like a tree planted by streams of water, which yields its fruit in season and whose leaf does not wither. Whatever [she] does prospers. Not so the wicked! They are like chaff that the wind blows away. Therefore the wicked will not stand in the judgment, nor sinners in the assembly of the righteous. For the LORD watches over the way of the righteous, but the way of the wicked will perish.

Do you notice a progression in those verses? First, you're just walking by a tempting situation; then it gets your attention, so you stop and stand to take a closer look. Next thing you know, you're sitting down with mockers. Sounds like the lure of the television, doesn't it? Boy, that's another battleground! You're walking through the family room, and a show catches your eye. You stand to watch it for a few minutes, and the next thing you know you're plopped down on the couch. Four hours later, you've got a mind full of mush, and not a drop of housework has been accomplished. Any Personality type can struggle with the television, but certainly those of us who like to have a good time need to stay on guard.

One of the most unattractive habits shared by many Popular women is the seemingly irresistible urge to "one-up" other people's stories. You may think this is a way of connecting, a way of communicating: "Hey, I can relate to what you are saying." But that's not the way others perceive it. Why not try a little experiment? For the next week or so, consciously stay alert to other people's perceptions of you. When you're in a group, your natural tendency is probably to shift into your performance mode and pay little attention to the nonverbal clues others send your way. In particular, learn the clues that indicate boredom: disconnecting eye contact, shifting from side to side, glancing at watches, looking around the room, and of course, yawning. Here's a radical idea. Launch into a story and deliberately stop midway through. You might be surprised to discover that no one asks you to pick up where you left off! In other words, they weren't that interested in your story.

It may seem impossible to you that anyone would ever be bored by *your* stories, but at least remain open to the possibility. You might be unpleasantly surprised by the results. If your stories tend to drag on forever, learn to get to the point. Well, okay, learn to get there faster than you used to!

Do you often regret your words? Have you ever played that game where you see how long you can keep your mouth shut in class or in a social situation? Have you ever written little reminder notes to yourself about keeping quiet? And yet, in spite of all your efforts, you can never keep quiet for very long? Somehow, you still manage to say the wrong thing at the wrong time? Here are some Bible verses to ponder. Proverbs 4:23 says, "Above all else, guard your heart, for it is the wellspring of life." Matthew 12:35–37 notes:

> The good man brings good things out of the good stored up in him, and the evil man brings evil things out of the evil stored up in him. But I tell you that men will have to give account on the day of judgment for every careless word they have spoken. For by your words you will be acquitted, and by your words you will be condemned.

The problem isn't with your mouth; the problem is with your heart.

Perhaps you've never thought of it this way before, but the underlying issue is a low regard for other people. Chances are, you have a tough time listening because you don't genuinely care about what anyone else has to say. When someone else is talking, you're busy plotting your next sentence or interrupting and finishing other people's sentences, even answering questions on their behalf. Do you, by any chance, answer questions directed at your boyfriend or husband? Admit it, now!

Pray that God will change your heart, giving you a genuine concern for the interests of others. As you do that, you'll find yourself more eager to listen and less eager to offer up pat answers or amusing stories.

Does that mean you should somehow force yourself to become introverted? Definitely not. God created you to be an extrovert, and there's nothing inherently wrong with being an outgoing person. It only becomes a problem when your heart is not in the right place. When your heart begins to overflow with the things of God—love, joy, peace, patience, kindness, faithfulness, and self-control—your tongue won't get you into nearly as much trouble. In fact, your words will become a powerful tool for blessing the world around you.

Focus on your heart. As you prayerfully and practically work to make changes, remember that the goal is not to become someone you're not; the goal is to become the best possible *you*. Here are some quick tips to help you achieve that goal:

1. *Use your personal popularity for good.* With your winning smile, vibrant personality, and natural charisma, you have tremendous potential to influence your world. So make a conscious decision about how you are going to use that influence. You might even sit down and complete the following sentence: "Because they know me, I want people to _____." Then fill in the blank describing the positive impact you want to have on people's lives.

2. *Throw parties for a cause.* Here again, you have a great opportunity to make a difference in your world, just by being you. I've always loved to throw parties, but rather than generic "stand around and goof off" parties, I host parties with a mission. I hosted a Nepali festival, featuring slides, a message from

an itinerant evangelist, and food from that region of the world. When I hosted a Moroccan festival, we removed the legs from our dining room table and put pillows around, and we all sat on the floor to eat while missionaries to that country shared their life and ministry with us. The truly brave among us even tried eating Moroccan style: with our bare hands! Then there was the Haitian festival and, well, you get the idea. Why not party with a purpose?

3. *Spread your creativity.* I absolutely love speaking at women's retreats, and I can always tell whether or not the Popular women of the church are using their gifts. (Every church has their share of these creative women; the question is what role they are willing and welcome to play.) I've been to some churches where you would never even guess that a special event was underway. But at other churches—wow! The creativity of the decorations is such a blessing. From the minute everyone arrives, we know something exciting is going to happen. We know someone cared enough to put her creativity to work. Don't let anyone tell you that your creative gifts are superfluous or unnecessary. Spread that creativity around and be a blessing!

4. *Reach out to the lonely.* Because you're such a natural people person, you probably have no idea just how lonely some women are. Believe me, I meet them at every church and in every city in America. Women who are overlooked and left out, women who are never included on anyone's social calendar. If only you knew what a difference you could make just by making one phone call per day to women whose phones never ring. If only you knew what it would mean for them to feel included or just to hear a cheerful voice. Look around you: perhaps there are lonely widows or lonely stay-at-home moms in your church or neighborhood. Reach out and touch them. You can make a difference in their lives just by being you.

5. *Be a motivator.* One of my neighbors, Ann, is a shining example of a motivator. When she started attending church a few

years back, half the neighborhood followed her lead. When she decided to join a small group Bible study, suddenly it was the thing to do. She is so excited about what God is doing in her life, and she shares it with such exuberance, that others can't help but get excited. You can do the same in your neighborhood!

=3=

INTRODUCING
THE PERFECT WOMAN

Perfect Strengths

Meticulous Housekeeper

The Perfect woman is often seen with her beloved companion: her trusty feather duster. These are the women who put Martha Stewart to shame, but then again, they're also the women who keep Martha Stewart in business, so I guess it's okay. The Perfect woman loves creating and maintaining the ideal home. She's usually a fabulous decorator and gourmet cook. She approaches household chores in a well-organized and self-disciplined fashion. Her motto is "A place for everything and everything in its place."

I remember attending a full-day home organization seminar taught by Emilie Barnes, the legendary Queen of Household Management. She absolutely captivated me with her ostrich feather duster, super-boxes, alphabetical card-filing systems, and cleaning-supply apron. It was obvious that she truly had a passion for housework. I used to think those Perfect women were big phony balonies. *No one's* that *organized*, I thought. *When no one's looking, I'll bet their houses are just as messy as mine. After all, even I clean up for company.* (In fact, whenever I start cleaning, my kids invariably say, "So, who's coming over?" The first time my daughter said that to me, she was only two years old. Just a toddler and she already had me figured out.)

But the Perfect woman is no phony. She doesn't wait until someone is coming over to clean. She genuinely takes great delight in keeping her surroundings in order. If one of your friends is this Personality type, you can stop by her house at any given moment, day or night, and guess what? Everything will be absolutely, positively *perfect*.

Of course, there is one major problem with the Perfect woman. When she moves into the neighborhood, she makes the rest of us look bad! Our husbands start getting wild ideas about home-cooked meals and ironed shirts. They want to know why *our* whites aren't whiter than white. (Just kidding, of course!) I have a girlfriend who is a Popular woman, and her mother-in-law is a Perfect woman. Her poor husband just can't understand why their house doesn't look like the one he grew up in. Based on what you've learned so far about the Personalities, what are the chances of a Popular woman's house ever looking anything remotely like the Perfect woman's house? The correct answer is zero!

Organized

The Perfect woman's organizational skills extend beyond her home. If she works—whether it's in an office, running a home business, or volunteering at the church—her desk will be in perfect order. In fact, a surefire way to identify this Personality type is to peek into drawers—the pens will be neatly lined up in one section, notepaper stacked in a corner, you get the idea. Her entire approach to life is organized: she plans her day and follows the plan. She lives by her calendar, keeps records of car repairs, invites you for dinner, waits for a return invitation, then invites you again.

She's the perfect person to turn to for advice on virtually any topic, from alphabetizing your spices to wallpapering the nursery, and everything in between. Chances are, she's got a shelf filled with how-to books and instructional videos covering do-it-yourself auto repair, cake decorating, dream home construction, you name it. She might even have a computerized system to manage the whole thing. This is no joke; I actually know a Perfect woman with just such a system.

She also takes a systematic approach to her family's health. Although she's a gourmet cook and can serve up sugar-rich desserts with the best of them, chances are she serves nutritious food for ordinary occasions. She may even be a health food advocate who takes an interest in alternative preventive medicine. No doubt, all family members take their morning vitamins, individually selected to address their physical weaknesses. If you aren't feeling well, call this woman for advice. For example, let's say you've been coughing. The Perfect woman will have a fifty-point, color-coded checklist to determine the precise cause of the ailment. She may be able to suggest nutritional or herbal strategies for preliminary treatment. Not only that, she'll be able to give you the name and phone number for the city's leading medical specialist for its treatment.

Perfectly Groomed

While the Popular woman sometimes has that just-rolled-out-of-bed look, the Perfect woman always looks carefully put together. In fact, the easiest way to spot this Personality is to study her appearance: neat, fashionable, well-groomed. Many have short, sleek hairstyles. I've theorized that this is so they can look perfect—even in the shower!

I'll never forget stopping by my friend Ruth's house in the middle of the afternoon, shortly after her second child was born. There she was, perfectly groomed and neatly dressed, from her head down to her feet. What stands out most in my memory was watching her change the baby's diaper and observing that her fingernails were perfectly manicured.

Before I understood the Personalities, I thought surely *all* women looked as ragged around the house as I do. (You know, funky old clothes, no makeup, hair in a ponytail—shower optional!) Well, I had never seen my neighbor Gayle looking anything less than perfect. So early one Saturday morning, for a joke, I turned on my video camera and began walking toward her house, narrating the whole time: "Ladies and gentlemen, we are now approaching the home of Gayle. We are about to discover what she really looks like—without her hair styled, without makeup, without any man-made accoutrements. Here she comes, she's opening the door, and she looks . . . absolutely *perfect*." We've now been neighbors for four years and I have never once seen her without makeup. Gayle told me she never leaves her bedroom until she's showered, dressed, and fully groomed.

Wonderful Hostess

On yet another occasion, I stopped by my friend Jan's house the day before her daughter's sixth birthday party. The theme was the Little Mermaid, but there wasn't a prepackaged Disney character in sight. No way! She was cutting out small white triangles, and I asked what they were. "Shark's teeth," she replied casually. She had made a giant shark and planned to photograph each of the party attendees peeking out of the shark's mouth. To get just the right effect, she was cutting out individual shark teeth by hand and gluing them, one by one, onto the handmade shark. Does this boggle your mind?

The party was, of course, fabulous. Jan hand-painted fish cookies with frosting in tropical patterns. There was a homemade mermaid cake. Not the kind with little plastic characters you pick up at the local grocery store bakery. No, this had a beautiful mermaid doll protruding out of the center of the cake.

For the adults, she prepared gourmet foods ranging from chicken and wild rice to sautéed shrimp. When she discovered that I had to leave early, she prepared a special take-home plate. There were all kinds of games for children and a luau, complete with hula dancing and limbo, for the adults.

The amazing part is, she entertains like this *on a regular basis.*

Detail Oriented

The Perfect woman actually *reads* the instruction manuals that go with her appliances, which is why her appliances last so much longer than other women's. She likes to do everything by the book and doesn't waste time reinventing the wheel. She wants to know the right way to do things and places great faith in what worked in the past. She's not the type to chase after every new innovation that comes down the pike, preferring to stick with the tried-and-true. In fact, the decor in her home is probably classic and traditional.

When the Perfect woman brings this characteristic to bear on her devotional life, the results are marvelous. She becomes an avid student of the Bible, she devotes herself to a regularly scheduled daily quiet time, and she systematically cultivates the spiritual disciplines that lead to a deeper Christian life.

Thoughtful

Though it's wonderful that the Perfect woman never overlooks a detail, what's even more important is the way her attention to details translates into thoughtfulness. She remembers birthdays and holidays with cards and gifts, and not the kind of gifts you grab off the shelf at Wal-Mart at the last minute. No, she gives gifts that were carefully chosen and purchased weeks in advance.

Caroline is a great example. In our neighborhood, we have monthly dinner parties called "Dine with Friends," where five couples take turns hosting dinner in their home. I remember one occasion when the hostess had asked Caroline to share one of her legendary recipes. This is no minor thing, people. You have to attend a training class and become certified, and even then you've got to sign a release form before obtaining individual recipes. (Kidding!)

Anyway, wouldn't you know the hostess overmarinated the chicken? So when her husband tried to put it on the grill, it went sopping through. When Caroline arrived on the scene early, in case her help was needed in the kitchen, she realized the hostess's dilemma and immediately sprang into action. She sent her husband to the nearest grocery store to buy chicken and gathered the ingredients to make a new marinade. She mixed it up and had it refrigerated for half an hour . . . all before I managed to *arrive* at the party.

When the hostess brought out the dinner plates (that Caroline had helped her arrange to look like something you'd be served in a gourmet restaurant), she reached to put a plate in front of me. Caroline softly whispered, "No, no, no. I've got Donna's plate right here. See, it doesn't have any mushrooms on it." I gave her a "How on earth did you know that?" glance, and she explained, "You left your mushrooms on the plate last time."

Here is a woman who not only noticed that I didn't eat my mushrooms at another dinner party, she actually remembered it two months after the fact. More to the point, she cared enough to do something about it. Wow! That's what I call thoughtful.

Frugal

The Perfect woman is extremely frugal. It doesn't matter how much money she has, she wants to spend it wisely. She may have enough money in her child's college fund to cover four years at an Ivy League university, yet she will spend four hours every week clipping seventy-five-cent coupons and driving to five different grocery stores in hopes of saving twenty dollars.

Grocery stores aren't the only place she wants to save money. Just this morning, one of my friends called to let me know about a new consignment shop she had found. She was overjoyed to report that she had bought four beautiful party dresses for twenty dollars. Her husband is extremely successful, and they could certainly afford to shop at the finest stores in town, but as she says, "I *hate* paying retail."

Careful Decision Maker

While some may consider the Perfect woman too slow in making decisions, she is simply cautious. She investigates every possible angle. If she wants to buy a new blender, she'll research the various brands online or in *Consumer Reports*. (Come to think of it, she might just have a subscription to *Consumer Reports*.) Often she can avoid problems the rest of us fall into because she makes wise decisions in the first place and averts problems before they begin.

Sophisticated

The Perfect woman is extremely sophisticated. Rather than Disney movies, she has her children watching classic films such as *National Velvet* and *Little Women*. She doesn't want her children reading the latest pop novel-turned-movie or movie-turned-novel; instead, she'll provide them with a reading list of great literature. In fact, she'll probably invest in those leather-bound editions of the World's Greatest Books. While the rest of the women in the waiting room read *People* magazine, she takes out her *National Geographic*. When she needs decorating ideas, she doesn't turn to *Family Circle*, she turns to *Architectural Digest*. (Here's a little tip: if any of your friends subscribe to *Architectural Digest*, you should immediately be able to guess which Personality type you're dealing with!) She loves the ballet, museums, and the symphony.

She wouldn't be caught dead hosting a potluck supper. Her idea of a simple dinner party is a five-course meal that features stuffed crab and various recipes from *Bon Appétit*. She orders her clothes from the Talbot's catalog or shops consignment chic.

Perfect Weaknesses

Perfectionist

Isn't it wonderful that the Perfect woman is so perfect? Wouldn't it be just dandy for a guy to have a girlfriend or wife like that? Then his life would be perfect, and everyone would be happy, right? Well, not necessarily. You see, all of this perfection can go too far and end up creating stress for the people around her. She sets unrealistically high standards for everything from household chores to academic and sports performance. She'll drive past ten gymnastic studios to get to the right one, even if it's thirty miles away. She'll hire the right coach and make sure her kids get the right teacher at the right school. In theory, that sounds wonderful. In reality, it creates an incredible amount of stress. Some women maintain homes that are so neat and clean, people are afraid to breathe. This can be a very stifling environment for a child, especially a Popular or Peaceful child.

Have you ever watched an event like the following unfold? You are attending a social gathering in the home of a Perfect woman. The food, the decor, the ambiance—everything is perfect. Even the white carpet looks perfect, until that fateful moment when someone spills a bit of punch. Now, it doesn't have to be a glassful of punch, just a little bit of punch. What happens next? With great fanfare, the hostess runs to get out her bottle of carpet cleaning solution and spends ten minutes on her hands and knees cleaning up every microscopic trace of punch. It's like watching her perform surgery. In fact, all other conversations cease as the unfolding drama becomes the talk of the party. ("What's she doing?" "Oh, really, who spilled it?")

It's nice that the Perfect woman wants her carpet to look great. The problem is that she seems to care more about the condition of her carpet than the feelings of her guest. That's perfection run amok.

Unpopular

Since the Perfect woman is very quiet and thoughtful, she can come across as cold and distant, which can make her somewhat unpopular. The reality is that she may simply be shy or fearful. Chances are, she has been hurt by disappointing friendships in the past and wants to guard her heart. She works tirelessly to ensure that everything in her life—her home, her relationships, her career or ministry—appears absolutely perfect. And it usually does from a distance. She doesn't want you to get close to her, for fear you might figure out she's not quite as perfect as she wants you to believe. She is often very guarded with her personal life and her emotions.

She's cautious in making new friends. After all, the perfect friend is not easy to come by. Should she allow you the privilege of becoming her friend, get ready for a package of E-X-P-E-C-T-A-T-I-O-N-S that Dale Carnegie himself couldn't live up to. She will expect you to listen to her endless tales of woe, told with painstaking detail. She'll expect you to know when and why she's depressed. When she's mad at you, she'll expect you to figure out why with hardly a clue from her. She'll expect you to remember her birthday and give her the kind of thoughtful gift she prides herself on giving. When you don't live up to her expectations (and the truth is, no mere mortal will ever be perfect enough for her taste), she can become extremely bitter.

Rigid

The Perfect woman can be quite rigid in demanding adherence to her many, many, *many* rules. She's got a rule for everything from the mundane to the sublime. From "Always put the spices back on the shelf in alphabetical order" to "Always load all the glasses in the dishwasher before you begin loading the cups and saucers" to "Always give solid evidence that you planned your girl's birthday gift at least three months in advance." There's only one right way to do everything, and she sincerely believes she knows what it is.

Once the Perfect woman sets the rules, she considers them set in stone. She can be a tough taskmaster toward her boyfriend or husband, her children, and even her friends. Unfortunately she sometimes gets so busy orchestrating life that she forgets to live life.

The Perfect woman lives by the letter of the law, not the spirit. I once put up a notice at a senior citizens' center that I was looking for a grandma "to hold my baby" while I tried to get some work done. Well, I got one response, and it was a Perfect grandma. She came to work for me, and guess what she did? She held the baby. Period. She didn't wash the baby bottles. One day she came to me and said, "There are no clean bottles." I responded that I'd been too exhausted (from writing) to catch up on dishes. She said calmly, "I'll just have to give her jar food then." And that's what she did.

It goes without saying that she didn't help with the baby's laundry or keep the nursery in order. I thought all of these things were implied, but I didn't bother to enumerate them. From her perspective, doing any of those other things might have involved putting the baby down for a moment, and the sign said she was supposed to *hold* the baby. What I meant to say was that I was looking for someone who would take care of all things concerning the baby. But not being detail oriented, I scribbled a very vague notice and tacked it up without thinking it through. The sign said "hold the baby," so that's what she did. She did it quite marvelously, I might add.

Prone to the Blues

The Perfect woman will schedule her day down to half-hour increments and see that everything looks great on paper. However, when her day doesn't work out according to plan, she often becomes frustrated and discouraged. Now imagine any mother of preschoolers plotting out her day and expecting it to go as planned! Basically, this woman is setting herself up for depression. And unless she can find a way to lower her expectations, she can make herself and everyone around her miserable.

She has to find a way to live with the unexpected, because life is full of unexpected twists, turns, and yes, disappointments. If she doesn't, her emotional life will present an ongoing struggle. More than any other Personality type, the Perfect woman is prone to the blues. Some are even given to despair, feeling that if life can't be as perfect as they dreamed it would be, they may as well check out early. Although no one has tracked suicide by Personality, I believe it's safe to assume that this Personality type has the highest rate. The alarming number of artists, musicians, philosophers, and other creative geniuses who have taken their own lives bears this out.

Understanding this fact has made me much more sensitive to my Perfect friends. I even have a fresh example to offer. Over the past several weeks, I've bumped into Martha on a half dozen occasions. Each time, I felt like she snubbed me, and I began feeling slighted. I started thinking, *What's up with her? Is she too good for me? Why is she mad at me?* Then an unusual thought entered my mind: *Donna, maybe it has absolutely nothing to do with you.* As someone who has always believed the universe revolved around me, this was a novel concept. But I began to entertain the idea, and it eventually took hold.

Sure enough, when I gave her a call, I discovered she had been depressed for some time. Unfortunately, I hadn't bothered to notice. Like most Popular types, I'm often self-absorbed. I talked with her for an hour and let her express her frustrations. I tried to offer her hope and encouragement that maybe there were some solutions, after all. Mostly, though, I offered a listening ear, and that's what she needed.

I had another Perfect friend I hadn't heard from in a few months. I'd been "too busy" to call her. When we finally did get together, she confided that she, too, had been struggling with depression for several months. Please be sensitive to this tendency in your Perfect friend. If you don't hear from her, take the initiative to reach out and give her a call. When she doesn't ask for help or attention, that's when she needs you most.

Unforgiving

In the same way she remembers every little detail about decorating and cooking, she remembers every little detail about what you've done wrong. More specifically, how you and the rest of the world have done *her* wrong. This is the type of wife who says to her husband, "Oh yeah, how about the time on July 9, 1983, when you . . ." and then goes into elaborate and accurate detail about the offense.

As a matter of fact (which, by the way, is a favorite Perfect woman phrase), she keeps a permanent mental record of wrongs, cross-referenced by offending party, type of offense, and date of occurrence. I actually read about one woman who kept a written record of everyone who had offended her. Can you imagine? Not only that, some women secretly like being wronged, because it gives them the opportunity to shift into the martyr role, which happens to be a role they relish playing. Unfortunately, it's not a role many folks like being an audience to.

I once read a prayer that shook me to the core, and I'll never forget one line in particular. It read: "A bitter old person is one of the crowning works of the devil." Doesn't that alarm you? That your life could become a living testament to the power of darkness, and all you'd have to do is become bitter? Perfect women in particular need to guard against giving the devil a foothold in their lives by making a conscious effort to forgive and forget.

Cheapskate

I spent the night in a Perfect woman's home once—a home worth more than a million dollars, filled with hundreds of thousands of dollars in furnishings from around the world. Perfect doesn't quite capture it. What a lovely, enjoyable experience, right? Not exactly. The place was absolutely freezing. And when I had to use the bathroom in the middle of the night, I was terror-stricken. (I can still hear my heart beating wildly.) Why? There was not a speck of light anywhere in this huge mansion. Earlier in the evening, the husband and wife had argued in front of me because someone left on the hall light for two minutes longer than necessary. (I felt like I'd entered the *Twilight Zone*.) Little did I know, they thought turning on lights was unnecessary. I'm talking total darkness here, people. I had to feel my way along the pitch-dark hallway, praying I'd stumble on a door handle before I stumbled down a flight of stairs and killed myself. Only a certified cheapskate wouldn't think to leave a light on for guests.

Making the Most of Your Personality Type

If I were a Perfect woman (and we all know I'm not!), the question I'd want to ask myself would be, "Why do I need everything to be so doggone perfect?" As you work toward becoming the best possible you, ironically, your first step is to lower your standards. That probably sounds contradictory, but it's not. In order to bring balance into your life, you'll need to come to grips with the fact that this is an imperfect world, where things don't always turn out the way you planned. Learning to accept imperfection from yourself—and especially from those around you—will liberate you from the bondage of perfectionism.

As you prayerfully examine your life, perhaps you'll discover that your greatest need is to cultivate a heart of grace and mercy. You might also ponder the implications of this verse:

> Why do you look at the speck of sawdust in your brother's eye and pay no attention to the plank in your own eye? How can you say to your brother, "Let me take the speck out of your eye," when all the time there is a plank in your own eye? You hypocrite, first take the plank out of your own eye,

and then you will see clearly to remove the speck from your brother's eye. (Matt. 7:3–5)

Keep in mind that the plank in your eye may be your tendency to look for the speck in everyone else's eyes. Romans 12:3 and 14:4 state this even more forcefully:

For by the grace given me I say to every one of you: Do not think of yourself more highly than you ought, but rather think of yourself with sober judgment, in accordance with the measure of faith God has given you. . . . Who are you to judge someone else's servant? To his own master he stands or falls. And he will stand, for the Lord is able to make him stand.

In case we missed it, God reminds us again in James 4:12: "There is only one Lawgiver and Judge, the one who is able to save and destroy. But you—who are you to judge your neighbor?"

Although God didn't create too many of us to become stand-up comedians, you may find your relationships enriched as you develop your sense of humor. It's sad but true: no one likes people who are deadly serious all the time. Your family and friends love you, but you sometimes make it hard for them to like you. Your toughest battle, after perfectionism, may be against depression. Perhaps the following suggestions will prove helpful as you seek to make the most of your Perfect Personality.

1. *Meditate on God's Word and pray daily.* Begin with the Psalms, especially Psalm 119:27–28: "Let me understand the teaching of your precepts; then I will meditate on your wonders. My soul is weary with sorrow; strengthen me according to your word."

2. *Count your blessings.* List twenty blessings or powerful answers to prayer on a piece of paper. Keep it in the front of your Bible and frequently update it as you experience God's miracles and even his small gifts. Review it daily until your heart begins to

overflow with thankfulness and joy. "Give thanks in all circumstances, for this is God's will for you in Christ Jesus" (1 Thess. 5:18).

3. *Boost your self-image by pondering all the truths about who you are in Christ*. Neil T. Anderson covers this extensively in his writings, particularly *The Bondage Breaker*. Don't believe your feelings; believe the truth. For example, did you know that you are a princess? Consider Romans 8:17: "Now if we are children, then we are heirs—heirs of God and co-heirs with Christ, if indeed we share in his sufferings in order that we may also share in his glory." If God, the King of the universe, is your Father, that makes you a daughter of the King—a princess. Pretty hard to get down on yourself in view of that truth, isn't it?

4. *Set yourself free*. Make a conscious decision to forgive those who have offended you, realizing that forgiving doesn't make their position right; forgiving sets you free.

> Forgive us our debts, as we also have forgiven our debtors. And lead us not into temptation, but deliver us from the evil one. For if you forgive men when they sin against you, your heavenly Father will also forgive you. But if you do not forgive men their sins, your Father will not forgive your sins. (Matt. 6:12–15)

> Bear with each other and forgive whatever grievances you may have against one another. Forgive as the Lord forgave you. And over all these virtues put on love, which binds them all together in perfect unity. Let the peace of Christ rule in your hearts, since as members of one body you were called to peace. And be thankful. (Col. 3:13–15)

5. *Stop looking for the gray cloud in the silver lining*. Choose to focus your attention on what's right in the world, rather than what's wrong.

Do not be anxious about anything, but in everything, by prayer and petition, with thanksgiving, present your requests to God. And the peace of God, which transcends all understanding, will guard your hearts and your minds in Christ Jesus. Finally, brothers, whatever is true, whatever is noble, whatever is right, whatever is pure, whatever is lovely, whatever is admirable—if anything is excellent or praiseworthy—think about such things. (Phil. 4:6–8)

6. Realize that depression is frequently biochemical. Consult your physician. Chronic depression is a serious disease and should be treated just as you would treat cancer, leukemia, or diabetes. Depression is not a reflection of weak character or a lack of faith, so don't beat yourself up about it. It may be a symptom of inadequate thiamine, biotin, B_3, B_6, B_{12}, or other vitamins or minerals. You may need to take a high-potency vitamin and at least two to three times the RDA of B-complex vitamins. Some physicians also recommend L-phenylalanine and potassium/magnesium aspartate (1,000 mg each per day). We all have our physical weaknesses, because we dwell in jars of clay. "But we have this treasure in jars of clay to show that this all-surpassing power is from God and not from us" (2 Cor. 4:7). Just think, someday God will deliver us from these imperfect bodies! In the meantime, we have to work with what we've got.

7. Be realistic. Let go of unrealistic expectations. Realize they only lead to disappointment, bitterness, and anger. This is an imperfect world filled with imperfect people. "For all have sinned and fall short of the glory of God" (Rom. 3:23). The good news is that we "are justified freely by his grace through the redemption that came by Christ Jesus" (Rom. 3:24). Jesus warned us not to expect our lives to be heaven on earth, but he also offers reassurance: "I have told you these things, so that in me you may have peace. In this world you will have trouble. But take heart! I have overcome the world" (John 16:33).

Pray the following prayer daily. Perhaps even commit it to memory.

Seventeenth-Century Nun's Prayer

Lord, you know better than I know myself that I am growing older and will someday be old. Keep me from the fatal habit of thinking I must say something in every subject and on every occasion. Release me from the craving to straighten out everybody's affairs. Make me thoughtful, but not moody. Helpful, but not bossy. With my vast store of wisdom, it seems a pity not to use it all, but you know, Lord, that I want a few friends at the end.

Keep my mind free from the endless recital of details; give me wings to get to the point. Seal my lips on my aches and pains. They are increasing, and love of rehearsing them is becoming sweeter as the years go by. I dare not ask for grace enough to enjoy the tales of others' pains, but help me to endure them with patience.

I dare not ask for improved memory, but for a growing humility and a lessening cocksureness when my memory seems to clash with the memories of others. Teach me the glorious lesson that occasionally I may be mistaken.

Keep me reasonably sweet. I do not want to be a saint—some of them are so hard to live with—but a bitter old person is one of the crowning works of the devil. Give me the ability to see good things in unexpected places, and talents in unexpected people. And give me, Lord, the grace to tell them so. Amen.

=4=

INTRODUCING THE
POWERFUL WOMAN

Powerful Strengths

I've got to tell you right off the bat: I think this Personality tends to get a bum rap in many books about Personality types. In listing strengths, the best one book could come up with was stuff like "puts projects before people," "doesn't consult spouse before making life-changing decisions," "doesn't take time for real conversation," and "is easily threatened by questions." These are the strengths? I was afraid to get to the weaknesses.

I may as well admit to having a personal stake in presenting the true strengths of the Powerful woman, because I am an even mix of Powerful and Popular. And as much as I love to have a good time and enjoy life, I am thankful God gave me the Powerful drive and determination to make a real difference in this world. If it weren't for my Powerful side, there's no way I could have written this or any other book. Books that, I hope and pray, have changed many lives for the better.

Take-Charge Woman

Women with this Personality do, in fact, have many wonderful strengths. Without further ado, let me introduce you to the Powerful woman. Here she is with her commander's baton, telling everybody else what to do! (Hey, wait a minute, that *is* a strength. Some people need to be told what to do!)

She is a shake-things-up, make-things-happen kind of woman. She is very energetic and outgoing, and she's always up to something new. As I've traveled around the country speaking at women's conferences and retreats, I've noticed that almost all of them are planned and coordinated by a Powerful woman. And I always quip, "I will personally guarantee that there are women in this room today who are here for one reason and one reason only: they were *told* they were going to be here." That always generates a good amount of laughter because it's so true.

Isn't it interesting that a Powerful *man* is praised to the high heavens for his leadership abilities, but when a Powerful *woman* demonstrates those same traits, she gets accused of being bossy, overly aggressive, and domineering? So often men consider her a threat while she is resented and judged by other women. Rather than supporting the woman who takes the lead, other women want to cut her down to size. I've seen this happen time and time again, in my own life and in the lives of women I greatly admire.

A famous Christian author with extraordinary leadership skills once told me that I shouldn't even bother trying to play a vital role in my local church, because the chances of my ever being accepted were virtually nonexistent. She said this based on thirty years of ministry experience, during which she had rarely seen a Powerful woman who didn't encounter constant opposition as she tried to exercise her leadership skills. You might think her words discouraged me. Quite the contrary! They were among the most liberating I had ever heard! They assured me that the opposition I was facing wasn't personal, but indeed, was virtually universal.

Powerful women, take heart. You are not alone. And the rest of you ladies, listen up: support the Powerful woman who's willing to lead. Be thankful she takes the initiative to get the ball rolling. Otherwise, most of you would be sitting home with nowhere to go and nothing to do. Thank God for these take-charge women!

Courageous

This is a lady with plenty of what New Yorkers call *chutzpah*. If you invite her to go skiing with you, she'll head right for the expert slopes. It doesn't matter that she's never been skiing before. She figures that if she sets her mind to it, she can do it. And very often, she can. Her motto is "Often wrong, but never in doubt!"

Some might say derogatorily, "She's got her nerve." Well, they can use whatever tone of voice they like; this lady does indeed have plenty of nerve that can be used in powerful ways for good. When a Powerful woman turns her life over to God, he can accomplish extraordinary things through her. No matter what needs to be accomplished, no matter what the obstacles, she will hold firmly to her belief that she can do it with God's help.

One of my favorite movies is *The Inn of the Sixth Happiness*, starring Ingrid Bergman. It's based on the life story of Gladys Aylward, a British house servant who approached the China Inland Mission in 1930 about serving God as an overseas missionary. They turned her down flat because she was not properly educated and didn't have any impressive credentials. But she believed God had called her and wasn't easily deterred.

She began saving every penny she earned and depositing it with the ticket agent at the railway station. She began reading all she could about missions in China and learned of an elderly widow, Jeannie Lawson, who was eager for someone to come assist with her ministry. Finally, she had enough to purchase a ticket from London, through Europe and the former Soviet Union, on to China. If this sounds daring now, imagine what nerve it took for a woman to travel alone to China over seventy years ago. Men did not dare go to the mission field without a mission society backing and supporting them. Even today, few missionaries would consider leaving home without a sending agency and without having their full support raised. This lady had courage by the ton.

In 1940, when the Japanese began bombing the village where she lived and worked, she led a group of a hundred children on a harrowing journey over rugged terrain to safety in another Chinese city. Let me tell you, there's not a Popular type on the planet who could survive in such a challenging environment. The Perfect types would have gotten too depressed to move forward when things didn't turn out perfectly from the start. And as you'll soon find out, the Peaceful type would never be caught dead bucking the system. When the mission society said no, she would have gone back to housecleaning and never uttered a word of complaint. But the Powerful type has the courage of her convictions.

Determined

The surest way to motivate the Powerful woman is to tell her it can't be done! Then watch her fly into action as she rises to meet the challenge. She views life as a series of problems to solve or challenges to overcome. Whereas most people will mutter, "If it ain't broke, don't fix it," she will shout, "Hey, if it ain't broke, let's break it and see what happens!" She lives from battle to battle, from conquest to conquest. That's why she often struggles after leaving the workplace to stay home with her children. There's nothing specific to accomplish; nothing is ever finished. I mean, as moms, wouldn't it be nice to be able to say, just once, "Yes, the work has been completed. The laundry has been finished once and for all." Let's face it, that just isn't going to happen. Although I have said to my family a few times, "*I* am finished."

Crusader

The Powerful woman not only notices the wrongs and injustices of life (which sets her apart from two Personalities already), she is compelled to set things right (which separates her from *all* the other Personality types!). She is the one who crusades for change. Powerful women can be found protesting outside abortion clinics, walking a picket line outside a convenience store that carries pornography, or serving as chairperson for a local charity.

After Deanna Allen's brother committed suicide in prison, she discovered a new purpose for her life. She decided to channel her grief into a campaign to reach hopeless prisoners with the hopeful news that God loves them and the outside world hasn't forgotten them. She has since reached out to thousands of prisoners and their families through conferences held behind bars.

Turning personal heartache into a public cause is a signature characteristic of the Powerful personality. If you trace the origins of many local, national, and even international organizations, you will often find they began when a Powerful crusader set out on a mission to make sense of something senseless that unfolded in his or her life.

Productive

Since Powerful women are so hardworking, goal oriented, and energetic, they tend to lead exceptionally productive lives. Many have successful, high-powered careers. As mentioned above, many—even those who believe strongly in the importance of being a stay-at-home mom—will crave more than just motherhood. It's important for you to discuss this aspect of your Personality with your man before the wedding and certainly before children come along.

I meet many women with this Personality who run successful home businesses or who head up various ministries or volunteer organizations. There's no reason to feel guilty about this, although some people who don't understand Personality types will try to make you feel guilty. Don't give in to them. That's how God wired you. He created you to thrive on getting things done.

My only word of caution to Powerful women is to be sure to listen to your heavenly Father's voice, so that you accomplish what he has in mind for your life. And here's a great rule to follow: if the work you're doing is from God, you should be able to accomplish it in a reasonable amount of time without neglecting yourself or the people who matter most. If your work is not from God, no amount of effort on your part will be enough to bring the success and fulfillment you're longing for. Come to think of it, seeking out God's voice concerning your choice of work and ministry is sound advice for *any* woman!

Recently I met a Powerful woman in Texas who organized her church's annual ladies retreat, for which I was the speaker. What a dynamo this lady was! And wow, what an incredible retreat! What a blessing to the hundreds of women who attended! At the closing, she spent twenty minutes thanking each of the women who played a part in making the retreat possible. She described what they contributed, called them to the front of the room, and presented them with gifts she had made herself. Then she made a comment that really grabbed my attention:

"God gave me a vision and heart for women's ministry many years ago. But it's taken a long time for me to learn to trust other women to do their part. I used to feel like I had to do everything myself if I wanted it done right. Now I know to just call the right woman and let her go. Let her do it however she feels is best, and it'll all come together." That's a hard lesson for many Powerful women, but once they learn it, there's no limit to what God can accomplish in and through their lives.

Open and Honest

You never have to wonder what the Powerful woman is really thinking or feeling. That's because she'll let you know, right up front, whether you want to know or not. She is the most open and honest of all the Personality types. Now, not everyone *likes* hearing the truth, but that's more their problem than hers. Often she has excellent insight that is ignored because someone didn't like the way it was presented. I think that's really a shame, don't you? The Bible says we should speak the truth *in love*. So, perhaps Powerful women could benefit from reading books such as *How to Win Friends and Influence People* to learn how to communicate more tactfully. Tact, by the way, is the art of making a point without making an enemy.

Interestingly enough, while the Powerful woman might get under your skin when she tells you one-on-one what she really thinks, I'll bet you love her when she says it from the podium or in the pages of her books. In fact, a majority of today's popular Christian speakers are this Personality type. Believe me, I've met a lot of them! And most of them made me look—and feel—like a quiet little church mouse. Usually they are a combination of Powerful-Popular or, hold onto your seats, Powerful-Perfect. Imagine a woman who not only wants it done her way *now* but wants it done perfectly!

I'm always amused when I get letters from women around the country saying how much they wish they lived near me and what great friends we would be. Here's a typical endorsement for one of my books: "I wish Donna Partow lived next door! Not because she has it all together, oh no, but because she is refreshingly, gut-wrenchingly honest. She minces no words, cuts straight through the masks, and opens her soul."

I have a feeling some of my neighbors might have a slightly different view of how wonderful it is to live right next door to all of my "refreshing, gut-wrenching honesty." (Just being refreshing and gut-wrenchingly honest with you!) Powerful women, keep in mind that open and honest is indeed a strength, but pushed to an extreme, it can become a weakness.

Effective Disciplinarian

The Powerful woman will carefully discipline the children in her life. Whether they are students in her Sunday school class or her own children, they are usually exceptionally well-behaved. She spells out exactly what she expects and carries herself with an air of confident authority that children respect. My good friend Jaime is a shining example of a woman who has her children under loving control. She has two daughters who are only eleven months apart, and they are the most well-behaved little girls you will ever meet.

She recently related this story to me:

When the girls were two and three years old, their absolute favorite thing was going to the library. Then we'd go home and I would read to them for hours and hours. On the way to the library on this particular day, I explained to them very carefully that they were not to run away from me. They were not to run around at all. A library is for being quiet. I told them that if they disobeyed, we would not be able to take any library books home. I made sure they understood exactly what I was talking about.

Well, we spent at least an hour carefully picking out thirty books, and the girls were wonderful. But then, just as we were ready to leave, they began running up and down the stacks of books. The librarian had just finished checking out all the books. I called the girls over and said, "Unfortunately, you disobeyed Mommy, so we won't be able to take any of these books home with us." I didn't raise my voice at all. I calmly walked over to the book return and stood there while they put every single book back. The librarian stood there in shock. The girls cried the whole way home, but they have never misbehaved at the library again.

I once asked Jaime what her secret was, how she got her children to behave so beautifully. She said simply, "I never give any warnings. I tell them the rules clearly. Then the minute they disobey, I nail them. It may seem harsh, but it's actually the most loving thing. When you give the kids warning after warning, or you don't consistently enforce the rules you've set, what you're really doing is training them to be disobedient. Then you end up angry and harsh because they become what you've trained them to be."

Well, Jaime is absolutely right. Of course, knowing that the Powerful woman is right (as she almost always is) and having the internal fortitude to apply her disciplinary techniques are two different things entirely.

Often Used Powerfully by God

Few books have affected me like *Give Me This Mountain* by Helen Roseveare, a woman who was used powerfully by God. I still remember the day I read it. I was home from work, sick in bed, and I plucked it off the bookshelf. I couldn't put it down. It recounts her experiences as a medical missionary to the Congo in Central Africa. I remember at various points shouting with joy and at others, weeping uncontrollably. Now here's what's truly interesting. A year or so later, I read a third-party analysis of her life and ministry in Ruth Tucker's book *From Jerusalem to Irian Jaya*. It talked about how much conflict and opposition Helen faced:

> Instead of establishing a regional medical center where a doctor worked around the clock and still fell short of meeting the needs of the sick, she envisioned a training center where nurses would be taught the Bible and basic medicine and then sent back to their villages to handle routine cases, teach preventive medicine, and serve as lay evangelists. It was a far-reaching plan, but from the start Helen was blocked at every turn by her colleagues, who believed that a mission had no business involving itself in training the nationals in such fields as medicine.[1]

Call me crazy, but it sure sounds like Helen had a brilliant idea. Nevertheless, she was opposed every step of the way by her cola-borers. Actually, that's quite typical for this Personality type. Very often, they have brilliant ideas and are absolutely right when they propose solutions to problems, but people don't want to listen to them or implement their ideas. Not only that, people often delight in actively opposing their plans.

Frankly, I think that's pretty sad, don't you? Okay, so some folks thought Helen was too pushy "for a woman." All I know is she made an extraordinary contribution through her life's work. I wonder how much the world misses out on because the ideas proposed by Powerful women are actively opposed?

Perhaps the most significant observation to make about the Powerful woman is that God chooses to use her in powerful ways.

Despite her remarkable sacrifice and great accomplishments . . . Helen left Africa in 1973 broken in spirit. It was a tragedy, at least in human terms, that her twenty years of service in Africa ended that way. [Nevertheless] . . . instead of bitter-ness there was a new spirit of humility and a new apprecia-tion for what Jesus had done for her on the cross. God was molding her for an even greater ministry—one of which she herself could never have dreamed. In the years that followed she became a much sought after internationally acclaimed spokesperson for Christian missions. She continues today to write and speak from the heart, and *her honest forth-rightness* [emphasis added] has been a refreshing breeze in a profession that too long has been stifled by its image of supersainthood.[2]

Powerful women, take heart. Though you may not be Miss Popu-larity, you're pretty popular with the God of the Universe. How's that for a trade-off? According to the Bible, no Christian should be surprised if the world despises him or her. To be unpopular for the right reasons is, in God's sight, a virtue. Nevertheless, being right is not the highest virtue; being loving is. Make a conscious effort, before expressing your viewpoint, to ask yourself not only, "Am I right?" but "Is this a loving thing to say and a kind way to say it?"

Powerful Weaknesses

Unpopular

As you may have noticed, the Powerful woman has many wonderful, admirable strengths. But they aren't the kinds of strengths that always endear her to the folks around her. Instead, she has the kinds of strengths that will be admired when she's dead and gone. While the Popular woman is making everyone laugh (so her friends love her) and the Perfect woman is maintaining a wonderful home (so her family loves her), the Powerful woman is busy saving the world (and who loves you for that?). Unfortunately, such impressive activities do not often lead to personal popularity. In fact, she may be greatly admired at a distance but disliked by people around her.

Mean

We're not pulling any punches here: the Powerful woman can wallop a mean punch. To others, she may appear angry, distant, and unapproachable, even when she's not in a particularly bad mood. She may just be so preoccupied with her own agenda that, frankly, she doesn't even notice you. When she *is* in a bad mood, boy, will you know it. And if it's you who put her in the aforementioned bad mood, look out!

When things don't play out according to her glorious vision, her temper can explode, wreaking havoc in its wake. She can be mean to her family and friends, co-workers, and even total strangers. This is the woman honking her horn and throwing a fit for the cashier at the local grocery store. She thinks the planet is populated by incompetent fools, whom she merely tolerates at best. This is a woman who can frighten people with her seething rage and bullying tactics.

She'll strike out and hurt other people's feelings with tough language and a harsh, unloving attitude. She may also use her mean streak to control her man, especially if he's a mild-mannered Peaceful man, which is extremely common.

Unfortunately, fear drives out love. "There is no fear in love. But perfect love drives out fear, because fear has to do with punishment. The one who fears is not made perfect in love" (1 John 4:18).

If you are a Powerful woman, you need to realize you are in danger of winning every battle but losing the war for your relationship. Take heed and try not to be such a big meanie.

Self-Centered

Have you ever been around a person who was interested in one topic—herself? I remember doing a large conference where the other speaker was a prominent radio personality. Having listened to her show, I knew she was definitely the Powerful type. All the speakers and behind-the-scenes workers gathered for a special luncheon, and this woman didn't say a single word. Not a peep! I couldn't believe it. The topics ranged from Kentucky Fried Chicken to world peace, yet this woman didn't comment on any of it.

Then it happened: someone asked her a question about a truly fascinating topic—herself. That was all it took. For the next hour, she talked nonstop about herself and bragged about her various accomplishments. No one else could get a word in edgewise. It was the old "Well, enough about me, let's hear about you. What do *you* think about me?" routine. It wasn't pretty. As Christians, we are to "do nothing out of selfish ambition or vain conceit, but in humility consider others better than [ourselves]. Each of [us] should look not only to [our] own interests, but also to the interests of others" (Phil. 2:3–4).

Uses People

When it comes to having friends, frankly, the Powerful woman doesn't have the time. It's not that she's incapable of being friendly, it's just that she isn't all that interested in the two-way give-and-take required to maintain a long-term friendship. She has her projects and her accomplishments, and that keeps her busy enough. Although, she doesn't mind leading a group (translation: telling everyone else what to do) or getting things organized and headed in the right direction (translation: telling everyone else what to do).

Notice we didn't say she doesn't have time for friendship; she doesn't have time for friends. There's a difference. She'll be only too happy for you to help her: she'll borrow stuff, ask for favors galore, and most of all, she'll call you to report her various accomplishments and expect you to make a big production over each one. The truth is, she tends to use people, viewing them as tools to accomplish her goals and objectives. In her mind, projects are more important than people—especially when they are *her* pet projects. This attitude inevitably leads to conflict. Here's how the Bible puts it:

> What causes fights and quarrels among you? Don't they come from your desires that battle within you? You want something but don't get it. You kill and covet, but you cannot have what you want. You quarrel and fight. You do not have, because you do not ask God. When you ask, you do not receive, because you ask with wrong motives, that you may spend what you get on your pleasures. (James 4:1–3)

Impulsive

The Powerful woman's ability to get things done is the envy of everyone in the neighborhood. That's because she doesn't hesitate to take strong action to get the results she's after. Unfortunately, she's often too impulsive in pursuing results. Let me give you an example. She'll wake up one morning and decide the living room needs expansion. Without any hesitation whatsoever, she'll march straight to the garage, take out a chain saw, and knock that wall down. When dear sweet hubby gets home, "Surprise!" Of course, if he's been married to her for any length of time, he's pretty much used to it. Now mind you, we didn't say she finished the project, she just started the project. Lest you think I exaggerate, I actually know a woman who did this!

Workaholic

In case this tendency to leave projects unfinished gives you the impression that this woman is lazy, let's set the record straight. Absolutely nothing could be further from the truth. Many are, in fact, workaholics. I'd better go ahead and 'fess up right now: "Hi, my name is Donna and I am a workaholic." When I worked in corporate America, I worked an average of sixty hours per week, even when I had the lowest job on the totem pole that paid zilch. Then I launched my own home business and really began putting in the hours. It wasn't unusual for me to work ten to twelve hours a day, six days a week. I remember one week in particular I worked more than a hundred hours. And when I relax, I often feel guilty.

You need to be aware that this workaholic tendency can place a very serious strain on your relationships. No one wants to feel second place in a partner's life. If you are constantly saying, "Not now, I'm busy" or "As soon as work slows down, we can . . ." beware. You do not want to wake up one day and realize you've lost out on love, or lost the love of your life, because you couldn't keep your personal and professional lives in balance.

Here's another thing I've realized about myself, and maybe some of you can relate: when I am not in my frenzied working mode, I drift into my coma state, conserving my strength for the big moment when I will be working again. Before I understood that I was conserving my energy for "important work," my own behavior baffled me and those around me. On the one hand, I was obviously a workaholic. Yet when it came to housework and the more mundane tasks of life, I suddenly behaved like a sluggard.

In their book on Personality types, *The Two Sides of Love*, John Trent and Gary Smalley refer to this Personality as the Lion. Interestingly enough, real lions sleep twenty hours per day. Did you know that? But when they *are* awake, look out. They spring into action and get so much done in those short four hours that they are considered the king of the jungle. What a picture of the Powerful woman!

Nevertheless, the Powerful woman needs to realize that much of life consists of the mundane. I love the way Oswald Chambers puts it:

> We do not need the grace of God to stand crises, human nature and pride are sufficient, we can face the strain magnificently; but it does require the supernatural grace of God to live twenty-four hours in every day as a saint, to go through drudgery as a disciple, to live an ordinary, unobserved, ignored existence as a disciple of Jesus. It is inbred in us that we have to do exceptional things for God; but we have not. We have to be exceptional in the ordinary things, to be holy in mean streets, among mean people, and this is not learned in five minutes.[3]

Bossy

Because of my writing and speaking ministry, I get lots of letters. I get crazy letters. I get heart-wrenching letters. I get wonderfully uplifting letters. And sometimes I get letters filled with correction and instruction from bossy know-it-alls. One of my favorites was from an elderly woman who opened her letter with the following:

"We were assigned to read your book for Sunday school class. As soon as I opened it, I turned to the woman next to me and said, 'This book is no good. See, she used the wrong Bible.'"

She then went on to critique my book, by page and paragraph number, pointing out everything she knew was wrong with it. From my spelling and grammar to my theology, she set me straight. Then at the bottom of the letter, in bold, block letters, she wrote a command (no time to even write *P.S.*): "DON'T ATTEND A CHURCH THAT HAS THE PROMISE KEEPERS."

We had never even met, but here she was taking charge of everything from which Bible I read and which preachers I listened to on the radio, to which church I should attend. And why? Because she knew it all. If you have this Personality, be alert to the fact that you can come across as the bossiest, most annoying know-it-all on the planet.

Making the Most of Your Personality Type

If you want to make the most of your Personality, your top priority should be coming to grips with whatever is driving your need for control. Did you grow up in a home where life was out of control? Perhaps you had an alcoholic parent? Pray that you will discover, deep within, that it's okay to admit you have weaknesses and that you don't always have the answer. People don't like know-it-alls, so why waste your time and energy trying to pretend you know it all? Only God knows all. Instead,

> Your attitude should be the same as that of Christ Jesus: Who, being in very nature God, did not consider equality with God something to be grasped, but made himself nothing, taking the very nature of a servant, being made in human likeness. And being found in appearance as a man, he humbled himself and became obedient to death—even death on a cross! (Phil. 2:5–8)

Although our culture extols workaholism, it is, nevertheless, an "aholism." It is not commendable. It is an addiction. Here's a little two-question test you can take: Would you rather work than anything else? Have you already lost or strained important relationships due to overwork? If you are out of control, you need to come back to center.

Let me give you an illustration that I hope will touch your heart, as it has touched mine. The city of Phoenix introduced a new technological breakthrough called photo radar. Here's how this little device works. If you violate the speed limit, it photographs your license plate, sends the data through a centralized computer, and then—get ready for this—they actually *mail* you a ticket. Now let's imagine you wake up one morning and realize you are late for an important appointment. You hop into the car and start driving like a maniac. You know the drill: as you travel down the road, you're digging through your purse for makeup. You put on your blush on the on-ramp. Then you get brave and try to navigate potholes and put on lipstick at the same time. You've got places to go, things to do, people to see! You do not have time to get bogged down in little details like obeying the speed limit.

Well, let's imagine you make it to your destination right on time and accomplish your objectives. All is well in the universe . . . until that fateful day when the ticket arrives in the mail. The point of the story is this: you thought you had gotten away with something, but you really didn't. You did what seemed expedient at the time, and you had no idea what it cost you until the ticket came due.

Friend, you might achieve all of your goals and not know how much it cost you until the ticket comes due. Like when your boyfriend starts questioning your relationship because you are frequently cancelling dates because "something came up at work." Not only do you need to slow down and smell the roses, you need to stop pushing everyone around you to work as hard as you do. Learn to relax.

Acknowledge the truth that you are not in control of the universe. Be willing to relinquish your need to control everything. Let God be God. And while you are on this earth, you must also be willing to submit to the leadership of others. Your natural inclination is to look down on all the "dummies" out there, but maybe it's time to admit that other people have gotten to positions of authority over you because (1) they deserve to be in a position over you, and (2) God placed them there.

While I'm on a roll here, you really ought to stop using people. You may think you are getting away with it, but people eventually realize that you are manipulating them for your own purposes, and they will begin to resent you. Realize that you are not naturally a people person, and make a decision to consciously work on it. Read Dale Carnegie's book *How to Win Friends and Influence People*, but don't use the techniques for further manipulation; really learn to value others above yourself. Part of valuing other people is withholding your advice until you are asked. Most people don't appreciate your advice because they don't like being told what to do by you or anyone else.

Florence Littauer surveyed her audiences about what one quality they most disliked in others. Guess what topped the list? Bossy. Then in a second survey, not one person in the audience admitted being bossy. That's because we Powerful types fancy ourselves as being helpful. We're not being bossy; we're rescuing all of those incompetent fools!

Florence says it best: "Powerful personalities love controversy and arguments and whether they play it for fun or for serious, this stirring up problems is an extremely negative characteristic."[4]

Stop arguing and stirring up trouble.

But if you harbor bitter envy and selfish ambition in your hearts, do not boast about it or deny the truth. Such "wisdom" does not come down from heaven but is earthly, unspiritual, of the devil. For where you have envy and selfish ambition, there you find disorder and every evil practice. But the wisdom that comes from heaven is first of all pure; then peace-loving, considerate, submissive, full of mercy and good fruit, impartial and sincere. Peacemakers who sow in peace raise a harvest of righteousness. (James 3:14–18)

Feel free to let someone else be right once in a while, and always remember: it's possible to be 100 percent right, but still be extremely unpopular. So take your pick: do you want to be right or loved? It's up to you.

Your aim should be to cultivate a heart of humility:

All of you, clothe yourselves with humility toward one another, because, "God opposes the proud but gives grace to the humble." Humble yourselves, therefore, under God's mighty hand, that he may lift you up in due time. (1 Pet. 5:5–6)

Read Andrew Murray's book *Humility*. In fact, anything by this wonderful nineteenth-century devotional writer should prove helpful. Consider the following gem of wisdom:

It is easy to think we humble ourselves before God, but our humility toward others is the only sufficient proof that our humility before God is real. . . . In God's presence, humility is not a posture we assume for a time—when we think of Him or pray to Him—but the very spirit of our life. It will manifest itself in all our bearing toward others. A lesson of deepest importance is that the only humility that is really ours is not the kind we try to show before God in prayer, but the kind we carry with us, and carry out, in our ordinary conduct. The seemingly insignificant acts of daily life are the tests of eternity, because they prove what spirit possesses us. It is in our most unguarded moments that we truly show who we are and what we are made of.[5]

As you cultivate that heart of humility, you'll have increasing opportunities to put your many talents to work. Here are just a few ideas:

1. *Take charge of a fledgling concern and provide the loving leadership needed to turn things around—or be bold enough to create*

something out of nothing! You have incredible vision and energy, so put them to work to make a difference in this world. Perhaps you can jump-start the women's ministry at your local church or launch a women's support network in your neighborhood. Where others see only obstacles, you have the power to see opportunity. Communicate that hope and enthusiasm to those around you. Let God do his work through you. I promise nothing in this world can bring you more joy and fulfillment than exercising your gifts in the center of God's will.

2. *Be courageous!* Even if you face opposition—as you undoubtedly will—you have a great opportunity to be a living example of courage and grace under pressure. As long as you are following where God leads and doing what he has called you to do, press on. In the words of the schoolmaster in the movie *Chariots of Fire*: "Discover where your true chance of greatness lies. Seize that chance and let no power or persuasion deter you from your task." Show the world what the word *determination* means!

3. *Crusade for a cause.* Even if there are no leadership opportunities open to you, you can still make a difference by crusading for a cause. Perhaps you can serve as chairperson for a charity fund-raiser. Pray first, then pick a cause you believe in and pour your energy into it.

4. *Stay productive.* Just because some women get tired even *thinking* about all that you can accomplish, don't be deterred. Take care of first things first on the home front, but if God has equipped you with extra energy, there's no need to apologize for leading an exceptionally productive life. Go for it! Change the world!

5. *Remain open and honest.* Cultivating a heart of humility will enable you to be the best possible you. As you live your life openly and honestly before a watching world, not everyone will understand. Some will be intimidated; others will pass judgment. It doesn't matter. As long as your heart is right before God, I promise your openness and honesty *will* make an eternal difference. A

verse that has greatly encouraged me is 1 Peter 2:23: "When they hurled their insults at him, he did not retaliate; when he suffered, he made no threats. Instead, he entrusted himself to him who judges justly." Isn't that beautiful? Don't worry about whether or not others misjudge you. Instead, entrust yourself to God, who always judges justly.

5

INTRODUCING THE
PEACEFUL WOMAN

And now I'd like to introduce you to a very special woman. The Peaceful woman doesn't draw *attention* to herself, but she does draw *hurting people* to herself. That's because hurting people sense that, in her, they've found a safe listening ear. Even total strangers tend to open up with the Peaceful woman, telling her about their problems and being comforted by her.

Peaceful Strengths

Comforting

When the Peaceful woman says, "I feeeeeeeel your pain," she actually means it. You're apt to find her, with her ever-present box of tissues, comforting the afflicted: "Oh, you poor thing. I've been so worried about you. You seem a little down lately."

She's the type of friend who will call you just to check in and see if everything's going okay. And if you ever need a friend to talk to, this is the woman to call. She's a very sympathetic listener, with a genuine concern for other people. She'll listen to your tales of woe for hours on end, without ever trying to fix you or top your story. She takes sincere delight in ministering to people's deepest heartfelt needs.

My good friend Denise is like that. She calls me at least once a week to ask how she can pray for me. Whenever I'm at the end of my rope and feel the weight of all my commitments crashing in, I invite myself over to Denise's house. I sit on her back porch swing, gazing at her flower garden, while she makes me a cup of herbal tea. If she knows I'm coming over, sometimes she'll prepare my favorite treat: raspberry shortbread cookies. What on earth would I do without this woman?

To tell you the truth, almost every one of my closest friends is this Personality type. I'm so thankful for friends who aren't the least bit impressed with "great" things I do for God. Instead, they love me enough to look me in the eye and ask how faithful I'm being in the small things. What a blessing!

Thoughtful

The Peaceful woman lives by the motto "It's *all* small stuff." And oh, how right she is! When my daughter Taraneh was about eight weeks old, I got a call from a Peaceful woman in my neighborhood. She offered to drive my older daughter, Leah, to and from Vacation Bible School for the week. As she explained it, "I remember the hardest time for me was when my babies were right around two months old. That's when the casseroles have stopped coming and the sleep deprivation starts to kick in."

Another Peaceful woman called to say, "My daughter has outgrown her warm school clothes. I thought of Leah right away. Would you like to stop over tomorrow and pick them up?" Not so long ago, the same woman had called to say, "I'll bet Taraneh is just about old enough to sit in a walker now. Would you like to borrow mine? My baby's too old for it, and it's still in great condition." You see, the Peaceful woman is always thinking about other people and what they might need.

Just before my baby arrived, my devoted band of Peaceful women really came to my rescue. One wanted to know if I was in need of a baby swing and car seat. Yep, I was. Another heard I was on bed rest, so she came over to clean my house and wouldn't take no for an answer.

As you can see, these are marvelous women to have on hand when a new baby is on the way. They are so wonderful at bequeathing you the necessities. By way of contrast, the Popular woman has no idea what she did with her old baby stuff. The Perfect woman isn't going to lend you her stuff because she wants to keep it in perfect condition in case she has another child or to preserve for her grandchildren. The Powerful woman is, as always, too preoccupied with her own projects to give much thought to your needs.

Attentive

Another one of this mom's specialties is note cards. How she loves sending note cards! These are the women who keep the *Current* catalog and currentcatalog.com in business. (The Powerful women are asking themselves, *What on earth is the* Current *catalog?*) They'll not only send you birthday and anniversary cards; they'll send you Thanksgiving and Easter cards. And cards when you sang a beautiful solo at church. Come to think of it, they'll even send you one if you *bomb* that solo. Cards when your child starred as the shepherd in the Christmas pageant. Cards just because she's thinking of you. In short, cards, cards, cards.

Here's one of my favorites, which I've kept for years. It was sent by the mother of two girls who were in my Sunday school class:

Dear Donna,

Just wanted to tell you that Julie and Kristi were very moved by your testimony in Sunday school. It's great for them to hear of the reality of life without Christ and the power of God to change people. . . .

95

It might be good if you could work out a way to have a confidential talk with Julie sometime. She had a bad "test" this summer—she failed. She's been weighed down about it. She just recently told me the truth. A talk with you might help her deal more completely with it all. Would you be game for a talk with her?

You are much loved by us all at [the church].

Joan

Notice that she's encouraging me for what I've already done. But she's also hoping I'll go "comfort the afflicted," which is actually a Peaceful woman's specialty.

Loyal

She's a very loyal friend. Once she's yours, she's yours for keeps. Janet was born nine months after I was, to a family down the street. We were neighbors for eighteen years, playing with all the same kids, traveling in all the same circles. Today we both live in Arizona. She talked me into it, in the quiet, persistent way that Peaceful women specialize in. What I think is fascinating is that people from our hometown—people whose names and faces I have long since forgotten—fly thousands of miles to spend time with their old friend Janet. These are the same people who don't even send me a Christmas card. (Of course, I don't send anyone a Christmas card because I can never quite get my act together on time.) You see, that's the difference between the Popular type and the Peaceful type. While I've gone on to have dozens of friends (which, I must admit, were really just acquaintances), Janet has steadfastly maintained deep, abiding relationships with a small circle of childhood friends.

At times, the Peaceful woman can grow discouraged, feeling that others don't reciprocate in friendship. Her Powerful friends are too preoccupied with their projects to give the kind of thoughtful attention she yearns for. My best friend—a Peaceful woman—turned fifty last month. Ever since her forty-ninth birthday, I kept telling myself I'd make a big fuss: throw her a surprise party, invite all her old friends, shop ahead for a thoughtful gift. Surprise! Wouldn't you know, I completely forgot. Meanwhile, her Perfect friends remembered her birthday, of course, and gave her the perfect gift in honor of the occasion. But they are too emotionally reserved to truly meet her need for close companionship. And it goes without saying that her Popular friends are too busy running off with the "friend of the week" to maintain a long-term commitment.

So, Peaceful women, you may need to find women who share your Personality type to meet your need for lifelong friendship. Of course, you can certainly hope that the man in your life will also be your best friend, but maintaining strong female friendships will prevent you from putting too much pressure on the relationship.

Peacemaker

One of the reasons the Peaceful woman can maintain such long-term relationships is because she rarely gets bogged down in interpersonal conflict. She thrives on harmony and will do whatever she can to maintain it. She's quick to adjust to the people around her and never insists on having things go her way. It is her sincere desire to please others. And not in the same way the Popular woman wants to please (that is, as a means to earn your applause and approval). The Peaceful woman is not thinking about herself at all. Quite the opposite, she's thinking of you and how much she genuinely wants you to be happy. Who wouldn't want to be lifelong friends with a person like that?

Often, when I speak at churches around the country, I'll be approached by a very low-key woman who is concerned about some conflict or another within her congregation. (All churches have conflict, you know.) Interestingly enough, while the Peaceful woman will not deliberately stir up conflict and will, in fact, avoid it whenever possible, she often feels compelled to act once she recognizes that's the best hope for seeing a peaceful resolution. She has a wonderful ability to see every side of an issue and to help others see their opponent's perspective. Her mediation skills are highly valuable in a romantic relationship.

Dependable

The Peaceful woman is 100 percent dependable. If she says she'll take care of something, it is as good as done. She's always there when everyone needs her, even though others aren't always as quick to meet her needs. In need of a babysitter? Count on her! Sick and in need of a casserole? She'll be on your doorstep with her chicken-rice specialty. This quality is particularly valued by her husband and children. They know, without a doubt, that she will be there during the tough times.

My friend Terri recalls,

When I was a senior in high school, I felt like my whole world turned upside down. My dad got a job transfer and, all of a sudden, we were living on the other side of the country. I had no friends, and I just couldn't get excited about making new friends, knowing that I would be going away to college in a year. The school was totally different—ten times the size of the school I had attended. I remember so clearly how my mom came to my room every night to see how things were going. And I do mean *every* night, without fail. She'd just sit there and listen. She must have gotten sick of my complaining, but she never let on that she did. When nothing else made sense, I knew I could depend on my mom to be there at the end of the day.

Protective

This is the kind of woman who sneaks into her children's rooms in the middle of the night just to make sure they are sleeping okay. During waking hours, she likes to keep her child on her lap if at all possible. I don't care if he's leaving for college! If she can get him on her lap, great. But she definitely keeps him within eyesight, that's for sure. I've noticed that many women with this Personality choose homeschooling so they can keep those kids in the nest and under their protective wings as long as possible. (The other type that homeschools is the Powerful woman who wants to whip those kids into shape and take charge of their education.)

If she does put her child into school, she'll volunteer to be in the classroom as often as she can. Why? Just to make sure her children are getting enough attention. When my daughter attended first grade at the local school, whenever I dropped by, I could count on the same group of women to be there. And let's not forget that poor, overworked teacher—better take her an apple. But if that teacher is smart, she won't dare criticize the children of the Peaceful woman. This mild-mannered lady can get pretty excited when it comes to defending her family.

Takes Time for the Children

Many of my Peaceful friends have large families. Beth has eleven; Barb and Sue both have five; Denise has four of her own, plus her three-year-old grandson; Christine has three but plans to have more. These are women who *take time* for their children, who sit and read for hours, who are not in a big hurry to go do something supposedly more important. These women resist the temptation to constantly utter my favorite phrase, "Not now, Mommy's busy." Three of them homeschool, which, of course, is just about the ultimate time commitment a mother can make. Barb's children came of age before homeschooling did. Otherwise, I suspect she might have joined the movement. Instead, she kept her children in Christian school, at great financial hardship, and always played an active role in their education.

The Peaceful woman is willing to chauffeur her children around town. Sue, for one, amazes me. She wakes up at five o'clock and starts getting the kids ready. She drives past the local public school on her way to a charter school twelve miles from her home. There she drops off two of her children. She turns around and drops off her teenage daughter at a top-notch junior high school, for which she had to obtain a boundary exception to enroll. She returns home and begins homeschooling her oldest daughter. At two o'clock, she again drives past her local public school to take her oldest daughter to the boundary exception school for photography class. Soon it's time to reverse the drop-off schedule, play pick-up kids, and head home.

Most of us would never do that much driving around, but this woman gladly will. (This Personality actually enjoys driving around. It's, well, peaceful.) Sue explains, "I just want the best for my children." She sure does. And she's willing to work sacrificially, day and night, to see that they get it.

If you are in a dating relationship, be sure you and your partner are on the same page about the number of children you want to have and the place of priority they will certainly have in your life.

Patient

The Peaceful woman is not easily angered. She doesn't even get mad when people commit the ultimate crime: obeying the speed limit. She's content to mosey her way through life in no particular hurry. She's willing to go with the flow and doesn't insist that things go her way. In fact, she'll quickly adapt her schedule to suit the people around her. "It doesn't really matter to me" is a common Peaceful saying.

The ability to adapt herself easily to any situation makes her a very appealing life partner. Indeed, the portrait of the good-natured wife who endures all things without complaint is really a portrait of the Peaceful woman.

Faithful

I never met Tammy Wynette, the 1960s crooner who sang "Stand by Your Man," but I can guess her Personality type. The Peaceful woman is loyal to the bitter end. Loyalty is her hallmark and the chief characteristic of her relational style. She has an exceptional ability to absorb emotional pain and still maintain her commitment to another person.

She will stick with a difficult marriage long after most women would have given up. I know women whose husbands were no-good bums—drinking, gambling, and womanizing—but the wives put up with it year after year after year. As you'll see in a moment, Peaceful women often marry Popular men, who are the most prone to infidelity. She'll forgive and hold the pain inside. Now, faithfulness can go too far and turn into codependence, but we'll save the weaknesses for the following section.

Part of the reason she puts up with so much is because she is a peacemaker who wants to avoid conflict at all cost. In addition, she doesn't expect people to be perfect and is tolerant of human frailties in others. Which isn't to say she doesn't have her limits! When she makes up her mind that it's over, brother, it is *over*. Period, final, end of story.

Kathy put up with all kinds of garbage from her husband for twenty years. Finally, she caught him red-handed in an affair. She pointed to the door and didn't listen to a single word of his protests. She had the divorce papers finalized within a matter of weeks and moved on with her life. Enough was enough.

Devoted Caregiver

It's not unusual to discover Peaceful women in the caring professions: teaching, nursing, counseling. A good number of them lead women's Bible studies or women's ministries. She won't be as splashy as the Popular Personality in leadership positions, but a faithful following will gather around her, and she'll have a highly effective ministry. She finds satisfaction and fulfillment taking care of an elderly parent, sick spouse, or children. She wants to please others, not as a people-pleaser but out of a genuine motivation and a heart that's willing to set aside her own needs to serve others.

She follows through on her commitments, as well. These are the women who will care for sickly relatives for years and years and never consider putting them in a nursing care situation, even if a doctor pleads with the family to do so.

I recently met the mother-in-law of just such a woman. At age twenty-two, this woman's husband, Heethe, was severely injured in a fifteen-foot fall. He had to learn to walk and talk all over again. The doctor told her that 99 percent of marriages hit with a medical crisis of this magnitude end in divorce. She quietly replied, "This is one that won't." Heethe's mother, Neicy, told me that she has rarely seen such loyalty, faithfulness, and dedication. "She's completely calm even when he loses his cool from frustration. She never utters a word of complaint as she bathes and cares for him. She has told me that the thought of leaving him has never even entered her mind."

The other person who has stood with Heethe throughout this ordeal is his brother, Jett, who also has a Peaceful Personality. (We'll be getting to the male Personality types shortly, but I couldn't resist sharing this here!) He was about to enter his senior year of college on a baseball scholarship, but he gave it up to stay home and help out any way he could. He quietly but firmly declared, "I'm not going back." Everyone was completely shocked, because they knew the incredible sacrifice he was making. A writer for *Guideposts* magazine called to interview him, and he was dumbfounded. He honestly didn't think it was any big deal. What a beautiful picture of the Peaceful Personality in action.

Peaceful Weaknesses

Unenthusiastic

Believe it or not, this devoted, kindhearted woman actually does have a few faults. Although it certainly doesn't seem like a weakness to her, perhaps the most annoying of the Peaceful woman's traits is her lack of enthusiasm. You can turn to her and say, "I climbed

Mount Everest this past weekend," and she'll say, "That's nice." And you're thinking, *She didn't get it.* So you repeat with greater emphasis, "I climbed Mount Everest!"

You can emphasize all you want. You're not going to generate much excitement. Her goal is to conserve her limited supply of energy. She's not about to squander it getting worked up about your latest exploits.

Now, this may seem like a small weakness. Some may not even consider it a weakness at all. But to Popular women trying to generate fun activities, Perfect women trying to do everything just right, and Powerful women trying to save the world, such reactions are like buckets of cold water in the face. This lack of enthusiasm can cause significant conflict in her relationships with those who have either the Powerful or Popular Personality. They may interpret her lack of enthusiasm as a lack of love and concern, which can actually result in emotional damage to her loved ones.

Uninvolved

Peaceful women insist they simply prefer to be in the background, but pushed to the extreme, Peaceful women tend to be too uninvolved. Yes, our families need to come first, but *something* should come second. Unfortunately, some women actually hide behind motherhood and use it as a justification for their lack of involvement. No matter what anyone asks her to do, the answer is, "No, I just don't see how I could." She enrolls her children in the local school, but doesn't want to volunteer for any fund-raising committees. Or she homeschools her kids, but doesn't want to participate in the local support group. She'll attend church on Sunday morning, but that's the extent of her involvement. She doesn't want to join a small group or attend the women's Bible study. Trying to get her involved is like pulling teeth! Whether it's a hobby, a political cause, a volunteer position, if you're a Peaceful woman, you might do well to reach out beyond the four walls of your house on occasion. Find something to devote yourself to, and do it with gusto. Do as the Bible says: "Whatever you do, work at it with all your heart, as working for the Lord, not for men, since you know that you will receive an inheritance from the Lord as a reward. It is the Lord Christ you are serving" (Col. 3:23–24).

Fearful

Part of the reason this woman hesitates to get involved is that she's fearful. She's plagued by "what ifs." *What if I volunteer to make a cake and it doesn't turn out right? What if I join the Bible study and I can't keep up with the lessons? Or what if the leader calls on me and I don't know what to say? What if I join this committee and people realize I don't know what I'm doing? What if it leads to conflict? What if some people don't approve of the new ideas we propose?* What if, what if, what if! It's possible to actually be paralyzed by fears and insecurities to the point that you never try anything new, never risk anything. Sure, it's safe, but it's no way to live. The Bible says, "For God did not give us a spirit of timidity [fear], but a spirit of power, of love and of self-discipline" (2 Tim. 1:7).

Other verses that should be of special encouragement to you as you seek to overcome that spirit of fear:

Strengthen the feeble hands, steady the knees that give way; say to those with fearful hearts, "Be strong, do not fear; your God will come." (Isa. 35:3–4)

So do not fear, for I am with you; do not be dismayed, for I am your God. I will strengthen you and help you; I will uphold you with my righteous right hand. (Isa. 41:10)

But even if you should suffer for what is right, you are blessed. "Do not fear what they fear; do not be frightened." But in your hearts set apart Christ as Lord. Always be prepared to give an answer to everyone who asks you to give the reason for the hope that you have. (1 Pet. 3:14–15)

Sluggish

The other reason the Peaceful woman is reluctant to get involved is because it sounds too much like work, and she is not very big on work! She's inclined to evaluate a situation based on the answer to this question: "What's the bare minimum I can do and still get away with it?" Then she'll do the bare minimum and not a drop more. If you stop by her house, you'll often find it not only disorganized (as the Popular woman's house usually is) but deep-down dirty. The oven has never been deep cleaned, because who looks in there, anyway? The bathrooms are rarely scrubbed, because that would require applying serious elbow grease. The dishes lie around for ages, and the countertops are eternally cluttered, because she's lounging on the couch watching TV.

In fact, TV can become a major downfall. She loves soap operas because she gets to experience life vicariously—all the romance and excitement without exerting a drop of energy. She loves game shows because she can imagine winning prizes without studying to learn any of the answers. And she loves the trashy talk shows because they lend an air of excitement to her otherwise dull life.

This sluggish lifestyle may lead to excessive weight gain, which may slow her down even more. Then the mere thought of getting up off the couch and back into life will become so overwhelming she won't even try. I've known women who've fallen into this vicious cycle. Eventually, they became so sluggish and gained so much weight, they basically dropped out of life. Don't let that happen to you. Throw that television away and set yourself free from its enslaving influence. Get up and get back into life!

Compromising

A Peaceful woman's noble desire to avoid conflict coupled with her sluggish nature may lead to some ignoble ends. For example, her inclination toward soap opera addiction will undoubtedly compromise her mental purity. She's a follower by nature and tends to compromise her standards to suit whomever she spends the most time with. If she's surrounded by dynamic, godly women and follows the crowd, she'll do well. But it's not likely that many dynamic, godly women are lounging around in this woman's living room every day, sitting idly by while she stares at the tube. With that type of lifestyle, she's inclined to attract the wrong type of friends—friends who drag her down rather than challenge her to grow mentally and spiritually. Maybe her soap opera buddies will introduce her to racy romance novels, and she'll become addicted to those, as well (see 2 Cor. 12:20; 2 Thess. 3:11). This can lead to a type of emotional adultery that is extremely destructive to your love life.

Recognize that you are a follower, and put that trait to work in your favor. Make it your primary mission to surround yourself with the type of women you hope to become, then follow their lead. You and your guy will be glad you did. It will involve getting up off the couch and taking some risks, but it will be worth it!

Enabler

Another one of the Peaceful woman's positive traits that can go too far and create problems is her faithfulness. (As with all the Personality types, her weaknesses are merely strengths carried to extremes.) It's difficult to say exactly when being loyal turns into being a doormat, but most of us recognize it when we hear the war stories. The words *enabler* and *codependent* became buzzwords in the 1970s and '80s, as we realized that certain people actually make it easier for alcoholics, drug addicts, and abusers to lead their dysfunctional lifestyles.

Although anyone can fall into the role of enabler, the Peaceful woman is the most likely to do so. I realize the following example may seem extreme, but you would be shocked at the stories I hear. One woman told me she had become an exotic dancer because her husband thought it was exciting to watch her entice other men. She knew it was wrong, but she didn't want to argue with her husband.

To avoid conflict and in the name of submission, she publicly humiliated herself. She finally drew the line after he invited men from the bar home and convinced her to have sex with them so he could watch. This man was an *elder* in the local church.

Perhaps you're thinking, "Well, my husband isn't an alcoholic and I'm certainly not an exotic dancer, so this doesn't apply to me." Maybe not, but I would encourage you to examine your relationship with your boyfriend or husband to see in what ways you might be making it easy for them to behave irresponsibly. Then lovingly, but firmly, back away and let him reap the logical consequences of his choices.

Making the Most of Your Personality Type

Okay, Peaceful woman, I may as well admit how partial I am to you. Virtually all of my closest friends share your Personality. But friends must be tough sometimes, so I'm going to lay it on the line for you. Girl, you need to drum up some enthusiasm! You can be so smug sometimes! You may not be considered a controlling person, but you've certainly learned how to control others with your lack of enthusiasm. Florence Littauer observes: "Once [Peaceful women] find they can upset others by their refusal to get enthused, they use this ability as a quiet form of control and chuckle under their breath at the antics the rest of us go through, trying to elicit excitement."[1]

As the frequent victim of this game, I don't think it's very funny.

How about this idea: try something new. Anything new. Even if it's just going to a different restaurant or ordering a different flavor of ice cream. Go somewhere you've never been before, just because you've never been there before.

Perhaps you've felt that you were better than the other Personality types because you don't have glaring weaknesses, but you should realize that laziness is strongly condemned in the Bible. Read through the book of Proverbs and note how many places it condemns the sluggard or lazy person while extolling the virtues of hard work. And in the New Testament, Paul writes:

> For even when we were with you, we gave you this rule: "If a man will not work, he shall not eat." We hear that some among you are idle. They are not busy; they are busybodies. Such people we command and urge in the Lord Jesus Christ to settle down and earn the bread they eat. (2 Thess. 3:10–12)

Sure, laziness is an inoffensive sin—the proverbial victimless crime—but it's a serious one in God's eyes. Check out the parable of the talents in Matthew 25 and notice Christ's anger toward the "wicked, lazy servant" (v. 26). God has given you time and talents to invest. He doesn't want you to bury them in a napkin.

Find some ways to motivate yourself. Maybe set some goals and ask one of your Powerful friends to torment you day and night until you achieve one. Hey, that's the kind of assignment she relishes.

One can hardly write a Christian book for women without referencing the dreaded Proverbs 31 woman *somewhere*. And guess what? It's going right here at the end of your chapter! Why? When I read this passage, what stands out in my mind is how busy and active this woman is. Yes, it mentions her inner qualities, but the vast majority of the verses focus on how incredibly hardworking she is. That's because hard work builds character. Just for fun, why not go through the entire passage and highlight all of the action words. God's ideal woman is productive, active, hardworking—you should be, too. A friend of mine in college had a saying you might do well to adopt: Life—be in it!

> A wife of noble character who can find?
> She is worth far more than rubies.
> Her husband has full confidence in her and lacks
> nothing of value.

She brings him good, not harm, all the days of her
life.
She selects wool and flax and works with eager
hands.
She is like the merchant ships, bringing her food from
afar.
She gets up while it is still dark; she provides food for
her family and portions for her servant girls.
She considers a field and buys it; out of her earnings
she plants a vineyard.
She sets about her work vigorously; her arms are
strong for her tasks.
She sees that her trading is profitable, and her lamp
does not go out at night.
In her hand she holds the distaff and grasps the spin-
dle with her fingers.
She opens her arms to the poor and extends her
hands to the needy.
When it snows, she has no fear for her household; for
all of them are clothed in scarlet.
She makes coverings for her bed; she is clothed in fine
linen and purple.
Her husband is respected at the city gate, where he
takes his seat among the elders of the land.
She makes linen garments and sells them, and sup-
plies the merchants with sashes.
She is clothed with strength and dignity; she can
laugh at the days to come.
She speaks with wisdom, and faithful instruction is
on her tongue.
She watches over the affairs of her household and
does not eat the bread of idleness.

Her children arise and call her blessed; her husband
   also, and he praises her:
"Many women do noble things, but you surpass
   them all."
Charm is deceptive, and beauty is fleeting;
   but a woman who fears the Lord is to be praised.
Give her the reward she has earned, and let her works
   bring her praise at the city gate. (Prov. 31:10–31)

As you seek to get in the game of life, let me offer you some quick, practical tips, as I've done for the other three Personality types:

1. *Actively seek to comfort those around you.* You have such an incredible gift for comforting; don't allow your natural reticence to prevent you from using it to the full. There are so many hurting people out there, and you can make a tremendous difference in their lives just by being you. Ask your pastor if your church has a Stephen Ministry. If so, find out how you can become trained as a Stephen minister. If not, encourage your pastor to find out more about this wonderful cross-denominational ministry, which trains laypeople to comfort others in times of need, especially during sickness and grief.[2]

2. *Translate your thoughts into action.* It's wonderful that you automatically think of other people's needs, but don't stop at thinking. If you think of someone who may need a casserole, bake it and take it over. If you realize a pregnant woman is probably in need of rest, take the initiative to help out with child care or housecleaning. Another ministry opportunity might be connecting women in need with those who are able to help out. In other words, you don't have to meet all the needs yourself. You'd be totally exhausted if you tried. Instead, when you notice a need—and I believe that God enables you to see needs that other people don't even notice—bring it to the attention of those who can help. You might notify the pastor or women's ministry leader. Or you might compile a list of women who say, "Yeah, I can make a meal once in a while." You could even

do it informally: "Barb, did you know that Susan's doctor has put her on bed rest? I'm planning to take a meal; would you be able to, as well?" Choose whichever option suits your lifestyle best.

3. Get on the mailing list for the Current *catalog or bookmark www.currentcatalog.com,* which features note cards for every occasion: birthday, sympathy, get well, thinking of you, and lots of all-purpose blank note cards. Again, I believe God will bring to your attention those who need a word of encouragement. This is one of your special gifts. Don't assume others will send cards if you don't take the time. Chances are, they won't. So have a supply of cards on hand, and you'll be a real blessing to others in your own quiet way.[3]

4. Maintain old friendships. Here is another of your special gifts and another opportunity for you to be a quiet blessing, just by being who God created you to be. Even if others don't always express how much it means to them, persevere in maintaining those old friendships. In a world that's always changing, folks are surely thankful for anything that remains constant, especially if it's the steadfast love of a faithful friend. Research shows that couples who maintain friendships with other couples have stronger marriages. Be sure to invest in couple friends!

5. Be a peacemaker. Although you are probably reluctant to jump into the fray when there's a conflict in your church or among your friends, recognize that you have a unique ability to bring peace. No other Personality possesses your ability to see every side of the issue and to remain calm in the heat of the battle. You can ask anyone in church leadership, and they will tell you how desperately needed your mediation skills are. Pray about it, and ask God to show you how he wants to use you. "*Make every effort* to keep the unity of the Spirit through the bond of peace" (Eph. 4:3, emphasis added). It goes without saying that keeping peace in your romantic relationship is priceless.

Part Two

UNDERSTAND YOUR MAN

6

HE'S THE POPULAR MAN

When I fired up my computer this morning and saw the blank page with the chapter title "He's the Popular Man" at the top, I knew exactly what I had to do. I called David. He picked up the phone and cheered enthusiastically, "Hi, Donna! What can I do for you?" The Popular man loves to brighten people's days.

You just can't miss David. He's out in the street playing with the kids, talking to everyone—and I do mean everyone, from little kids to grandmas—who passes by, laughing and joking, and always, always, telling stories. There are some folks whose Personalities are hard to read. But you can spot the Popular man a mile away. First, he's loud. He has a loud voice, and he wears loud clothes. Even if he's required to wear a blue suit to work, he'll don Mickey Mouse suspenders underneath. Second, he's open. His mouth is open, his arms are open to give out a bear hug or a back clasp, and his life is an open book. He'll tell you more than you ever wanted to know about his wife or girlfriend, his kids, his career, his childhood, and of course, his favorite sports teams.

Popular Strengths

Fires Up the Troops

The first thing you notice about the Popular man is that he just oozes enthusiasm. It doesn't matter if he's psyched up about taking out the garbage, he'll have all the men in the neighborhood convinced that trash day is the event of the season. If it's something genuinely exciting, look out! David relates how he fired up the neighborhood troops to attend a major men's conference:

Life was good. I didn't have any particular problems. I had a great marriage and a great family. I had a great job. But I still felt like something was missing. I heard about Promise Keepers, and it sounded interesting. I remember walking into the stadium on Friday night and seeing sixty thousand other men. That says it all. Wow. We were all there for the same reason. We want to get better. It was incredible to see all the men going forward on the altar call. It was overwhelming. [I realized] I'm not the only guy who wants to be a better dad, a better husband.

I came back all fired up and called my pastor. "Man, I've got to tell you about this." So on Sunday morning, he let me tell the whole congregation. I said, "We ought to get together and start a men's group right here in the church." Next thing, everybody's coming up to me after church.

We planned to meet at IHOP [International House of Pancakes] the next Friday morning. Five guys showed up that first morning. The next week we had ten. The next week we were at fifteen. I just kept telling everyone, "You've got to come." Pretty soon, we had so many people, we had to divide into two groups.

Then I hooked up with my neighbor Bob. We both knew what a difference accountability had made in our lives and wanted to get more men involved. Bob owns an RV dealership, and he came up with the idea of getting a bunch of guys together in the RVs and driving to the next men's conference in Los Angeles. We just talked it up wherever we went. I made a list of guys I thought might want to go. Some I called. Others I watched for opportunities to bring it up.

As a result, thirty men from David's neighborhood went to a men's conference in four RVs. It was the talk of the town. One woman who didn't normally attend church commented, "I don't know what your church is teaching, but my husband's been sweeping the floor every night. I think I like your church!"

Thank heaven, the Popular man can fire up the troops.

Great Salesman

Not surprisingly, David also happens to be one of the top sales representatives for his company. David couldn't resist telling me a couple of stories, which I can't resist telling you. For Halloween, he sends his customers a "boo bucket" full of candy with a note reading, "I'm trying to scare up some sales." On other occasions, "just out of the blue," as he puts it, he sends customers a bucket filled with jelly beans and a note: "I hope your sales have BEAN good."

David's networking savvy also explains why everyone in the neighborhood wears his company's brand of shoes. I remember the most recent occasion when I realized the Partow clan was in need of new sneakers. I called David and asked if I could come over and shop from his garage supply. "Sure, come on over at nine thirty. Trudy and her kids are coming, too."

Well, we had a good time trying on sneakers in his living room, with David cracking jokes and chasing the kids around the whole time. I asked him how a particular pair of sneakers looked on me, and he exclaimed: "You look ten pounds lighter and two inches taller!" I bought them. This guy could sell heaters in Phoenix . . . in August.

Great Family Motivator

Another of my favorite Popular men is Rolf. He does an extraordinary job of motivating and encouraging his children. He is, quite simply, the most wonderful dad I've ever seen in action. He is so loving, affectionate, and affirming. There's not a shadow of doubt in his kids' minds that their dad thinks they are the most talented, wonderful people in the whole world. And I guess that explains where his kids are today.

When they immigrated to the United States, the children were four, six, and seven. They didn't speak a word of English, and they lived in absolute poverty. They suffered severe financial hardships, year after year. But do you think they sat around with glum faces, feeling sorry for themselves? Do you think they sat around looking for someone to blame or pleading for government assistance? Not at all! They were the richest family I've ever known—if you measure riches in love and laughter. Rather than driving them apart, the hard times pulled them closer together.

Each night after school, Rolf would cheer the children on toward excellence in their homework. Did you ever hear someone cheering about algebra? It's quite amusing! He couldn't land a nine-to-five job, so he constantly thought up moneymaking ideas. (The Popular man makes a great entrepreneur-salesperson and likes to hop from job to job.) Since he loved having a good time, he decided to become a disc jockey. And he was so excited about having his own business and being a DJ, the *kids* got excited about having their own business and being DJs.

Today the children are sixteen, eighteen, and nineteen. They work side by side with their dad in the DJ business on the weekends. The two oldest are now launching out and doing their own gigs for school events. All three are at the top of their class in one of California's finest high schools. The oldest son, Dean, was just awarded a full college scholarship and plans to go into medicine. They've recently bought a house, and their future looks bright. I give plenty of credit to Rolf's incredibly hardworking wife. She worked day and night to keep the family afloat financially. But it was Rolf who kept the children's spirits alive and motivated them to believe that "in America, you can become whatever you want."

The Popular man motivates and inspires his family.

Popular Weaknesses

Haphazard

When it comes to home improvements—or anything else requiring attention to detail or actually reading an instruction manual—this man is in a heap o' trouble. This is a serious deficit on Christmas Eve when you're confronted with all those toys labeled "some assembly required." I mentioned this little weakness to David, and he immediately launched into the following story:

We had these tannish brown light socket things. I guess they're called outlets or something. I wanted to change them all to white. Not exactly a big deal. Unscrew a few screws. I figured I could handle this project. Of course, I had to turn all the electricity off first. On one of them, I didn't exactly hook it back up correctly. I went to turn the power back on, and it shorted out the electricity in the entire house.

Then he added very casually, ". . . and it was on Thanksgiving." I just about fell off my chair. Of *course* the Popular man would pull this stunt on Thanksgiving! When else? The saga continues:

We were having company. And I don't know if you know this or not, but not many electricians work on Thanksgiving. So there we were: no heat, no Thanksgiving dinner, and company a-comin'. The worst part was that not even the porch light worked. I mean I really blew the whole thing out. We were afraid people couldn't find our house, 'cause you couldn't see the house number. It was starting to get cold in the house. I walked up and down the street and asked every neighbor what they knew about electricity. It turned out that the uncle of a cousin's something or another had missed his flight. He wasn't even supposed to be there. Thank God he was.

Meanwhile, back at the house, you can imagine what his wife was going through. So I asked David what on earth possessed him to undertake this home improvement project in the midst of preparing for Thanksgiving dinner guests. To which he replied, quite predictably, "Oh, I had some free time on my hands. Hey, I had the day off. I wanted to do a project."

Ladies, I did not put a single word in that man's mouth.

Poor Money Manager

Although the Popular man is usually lots of laughs, you might not be laughing on your way to the bank as you try to cover yet another series of bounced checks. I asked Dan, another of my favorite Popular men, if he ever gets into trouble for spending money, and he said, "Oh yeah! On a daily basis. But I usually have a good explanation."

Women often discover after marriage that their Popular husband spends money like it's going out of style. He may even drive the poor family into bankruptcy, but on the bright side, he can provide free entertainment in the midst of it. If your man has this Personality, and if you haven't done so already, take the credit cards away from the man! And take over the checkbook while you're at it. You may as well take over paying those bills, too, if you expect them to be paid on time. Although there are certainly exceptions, most Popular men are terrible money managers.

Part of the problem is that he's just lousy at details. Stuff like math makes his head spin. Besides, money management just isn't that much fun. And part of it is that he loves to dress stylishly, drive a flashy car, and have all the right sports gear—all of which costs money, which he may or may not have. Unfortunately, he's not about to let a little detail like lack of funds stand in the way of his good time.

As one Popular man put it: "My wife thinks I'm crazy for spending sixty dollars on NFL jerseys for the kids, when we could get sweatshirts at Kmart for ten dollars. But I figure, 'Hey, the kids have to look good.'"

He tends to be an impulse buyer and likes to buy double of what's needed in the toy department. If his wife sends him to buy a Hot Wheels car, he'll come back with a six pack of Hot Wheels and a track. And not just any old track but the one with the big loop-de-loop. One man admitted, "Just the other day, my wife calculated that I've spent over seven hundred dollars on Thomas the Tank Engine trains. I told her I bought the entire set because one day it may be a collector's item, but I actually didn't think that much about it at the time. I was just having fun in the toy department."

He may also give way to impulse spending on large-ticket toys like cars, trucks, and boats. My friend Diane recently spent five days visiting her sister. When she returned, there was a brand-new truck in the driveway. Her husband, who has been out of work for nearly a year, just happened to be driving by the car dealership, and the next thing he knew, he was the proud owner of the latest make and model. The truck was eventually repossessed because they couldn't make the monthly payments.

I recognize that some Christian marriage counselors insist that the husband handle the family finances, regardless of Personality type. What foolishness! Whichever partner is best suited to the task should handle it. The fact that a woman writes checks and balances a checkbook does not mean she's usurping her husband's authority. It simply means she is helping him and the family by using her God-given talents.

Poor Judge of Character

Because the Popular man is an eternal optimist who always expects the best of people, he tends to be a poor judge of character. There is nothing false in him, so he doesn't see through the false masks of pretenders. As a result, con men, false teachers, and other unscrupulous people can take him in. I'm convinced that the Popular types of our nation single-handedly keep the late-night infomercial business booming.

Jake, a man who had been raised in a Jewish home and later converted to Christianity, was extremely devoted to his church and especially to its dynamic pastor. He served as a deacon and spent many long hours serving alongside his pastor. He trusted him. He believed in him. Then one day, the pastor ran off with the piano player. Jake was shattered. I'll never forget what he said to me: "I attended synagogue for forty years, and the rabbi never ran off with anyone. I still believe Jesus is the Messiah, but I don't want anything to do with the church."

Like most Popular types, Jake didn't remain discouraged permanently. As a natural-born optimist, he was able to find a new church and, after a period of healing, became just as enthusiastic about his new pastor as he had been about his unfaithful leader. However, it is possible for these men to get burned so many times they end up cynical. Nothing could be more unfortunate. You see, if he gives way to cynicism, he will lose the very quality—that winsome, trusting nature—that attracts people to him and makes him unique.

Prone to Wander

People often wonder why we hear so many stories about the pastor running off with the piano player. Once you understand the Personalities, you'll see why it's not so surprising after all.

It all begins when a dynamic, entertaining young man (obviously the Popular type) realizes his storytelling flair enables him to make the Bible come to life. People flock to attend his Sunday school class or small group to be entertained by him. He decides to become a pastor and attracts a large congregation with his lively, inspiring sermons. Life is fun and all is well. He marries a Perfect wife, and it's even better.

Then the burden of actually running a church begins to weigh on him. It requires attention to details. It requires listening endlessly to people's problems. It requires mediating conflicts and sitting in on long, dull meetings. Not one of these things is within his realm of strengths. The pressure begins to mount. This isn't what he thought being a pastor would be all about. He feels like a failure. Meanwhile, his Perfect wife is perfectly miserable with this flake of a husband she married. She criticizes him day and night. Life isn't fun anymore. No one appreciates him. No one accepts him for who he is . . . except, of course, the piano player.

More than any other Personality, the Popular husband is prone to wander. The following section explains why.

What Your Popular Man Needs Most from You

As if you don't know this already, your man's battle cry is "Let's do it the fun way." What you may not realize are his greatest emotional needs: attention, affection, approval, and acceptance.[1] When his needs aren't met, this normally fun-loving guy can become severely depressed. Here are some ways you can be sensitive to his needs.

Attention

The Popular man has a burning need to be the center of attention. He wants you to listen to his stories and laugh along, even if you've heard them a million times. When he gets home from work, he wants to tell you all the incredible things that happened that day. Incredible stuff always happens to the Popular man. He's an odd-experiences magnet. If you want him to feel loved, take time to sit down and listen.

In addition to desiring his woman's attention, he actively seeks to draw outsiders' attention to himself. If you constantly criticize him for telling stories or exaggerating too much, you may eventually wear down his natural optimism and take the wind out of his sails. You may think, *Oh great, he's finally getting serious and quieting down a bit*, and you'll feel like you have fixed him. But you'll be in for a very disappointing surprise. Rather than developing the strengths of the other Personality types (which all your criticism is intended to do), he will develop the weaknesses of the other Personalities.

Depending on which way you try to push him, he may become negative and depressed like the Perfect man, unmotivated like the Peaceful man, or an unavailable workaholic like the Powerful man.

Rather than trying to get your man to become something he is not, accept him for who he is. Yes, he is disorganized and loud and gullible. Yes, he is too trusting, and yes, it would be just dandy if he could get organized and pay attention to details. But if you keep beating up on him, I promise that you will not like the results.

For years, Joanna worked relentlessly to get her husband, Dan, to sit down and shut up. She constantly reminded him of verses in the Bible about controlling his tongue. When they returned from a social event where Dan had been the life of the party, Joanna would punish him with disapproval and silence. Eventually he learned to force himself to keep quiet when he had something *nice* to say. In those instances, Dan discovered he really could manage to hold his tongue. But when he had something negative or thoughtless to say, he still couldn't hold his tongue.

Think about the implications of this for a minute. Previously, Dan talked *all* the time. He told lots of funny stories and jokes and was tons of fun to be around. Sure, once in a while, he'd put his foot in his mouth or say something people didn't appreciate hearing. But people forgave his little slipups because all the cute, endearing things he said counterbalanced the bad.

What happened when Dan stopped telling jokes and stories and only spoke up when he absolutely couldn't hold his tongue another minute? The only things people ever heard him say were the little slipups. As a result, he gradually became extremely unpopular. Now, for the Popular type, this is a fate worse than death. The change took place gradually, over the course of many years. By the end of that time, he was a withdrawn, angry person. The once buoyant, self-confident man had become socially insecure. The former partygoer now holed up in his office day after day, working around the clock. A family who previously hosted guests in their home at least twice a week now never opened their doors to show hospitality.

The truth finally dawned on this couple when they took the Personality test and Dan revealed almost all of the weaknesses of the Perfect man: bashful, unforgiving, resentful, insecure, unpopular, pessimistic, alienated, withdrawn, depressed, loner, and so forth. They couldn't believe it! He had none of the strengths, and they both knew he was not a Perfect type. In short, his personality had been seriously damaged.

This couple is now working to rebuild Dan's personal confidence and to piece the fragments of his God-given personality back together. A significant part of this emotional damage was caused by a wife who constantly beat up on her husband, demanding that he shape up and shut up. Please don't do this to your guy. Instead, focus on his strengths—pray daily that God will help him overcome his weaknesses, and strive to meet his heartfelt need for attention.

Am I saying these problems are all the woman's fault, and the husband or boyfriend is just a poor, helpless victim of this awful woman? Definitely not. He's an adult, capable of making his own choices. Nor do I want to discount the fact that his behavior was genuinely offensive to her. If I were writing a book for men, I'd be coming down hard on his tendency to embarrass his wife and run roughshod over her needs for stability and dignity. But, ladies, I'm writing to you! You may not be able to change your man into the person you want him to be (we've all tried, haven't we?), but with the power of God on your side, you can work prayerfully to bring about changes in your own heart and mind.

Affection

This need should not require much amplification! Your husband needs lots of hugs and kisses. This can be a problem since he usually marries a Perfect wife who is not naturally affectionate. Well, start with cheek kisses. Even if it will mean smudging your makeup or rumpling your perfectly ironed clothes, give that man a hug!

Approval

If your husband or boyfriend landed in a sales job, he's probably quite successful. But if he is in a job that requires attention to detail or other skills he lacks, he may be feeling like a failure. Even if he's not the president of the company, he wants to know you approve of his career and his accomplishments. Praise him for closing the sale or maybe just for bringing home a paycheck week after week.

If you withhold your approval, your man will find people who *will* approve of him, even if that means giving in to office peer pressures, to which he is extremely susceptible anyway. He'll become "one of the guys," drinking and flirting with the women in the office. He'll become the kind of man who praises the Lord enthusiastically at church (because that's what brings approval), then spews out profanities at the office (again, because that's what brings approval). By giving him your approval, you'll be helping him overcome those weaknesses.

Acceptance

This is, by far, your man's deepest need. He absolutely, positively needs to know you accept him, warts and all. Rather than criticizing him and judging him for his weaknesses, *help him*. Help him organize the garage and his closets. Go into his office on the weekend (maybe once a quarter) and help him organize his work, as well. Keep a copy of his calendar at home and call him with reminders, if he'd like you to.

Now, if you do this with a servant's heart rather than a nagging voice, he will love you all the more for it. He will realize how much he needs you and how lucky he is to have you. The key, though, is to help in a helpful way. If he feels like you are bossing him around, you can bet he won't appreciate it. But if he sees that you accept him for who he is and just want to help him out, your efforts will endear you to him.

If he doesn't get acceptance from you, don't be surprised if he looks for it elsewhere. He might just spend all his time at work or playing basketball with his buddies. He may even hang out at the local bar "where everybody knows his name." Now, if you're married and you and your husband are both Christians yet he is hanging out at the bar, naturally a red flag will go up. But remember to look for more subtle indications that your husband's needs are being met outside the home. For example, if he spends an inordinate percentage of his free time volunteering at the church or being scoutmaster extraordinaire, he may not be getting enough of your attention, approval, or acceptance. If your husband constantly looks for excuses to be anywhere but home with you, take time to reflect on your relationship. Is it possible that he feels you don't truly accept him as he is?

I don't want to alarm you unnecessarily, and I certainly don't mean to imply that every Popular husband in America is rushing headlong into adultery. However, I think it would be irresponsible of me *not* to put you on guard to a significant emotional need your husband has. I've counseled enough hurting women to know that it's not uncommon for an emotionally hurting Popular man to turn to another woman for the attention, affection, approval, and acceptance he longs for.

Of course, you should encourage him to grow—mentally, spiritually, and relationally. You love him too much to let him settle for the status quo. You want him to be the best he can be for his own sake, but you accept him as he is and assure him that you love him in spite of his imperfections. God has given you a fun guy, so enjoy your life together!

=7=

HE'S THE PERFECT MAN

Do you have a husband oozing with talent? A very sensitive, self-sacrificing boyfriend? A faithful man who never pushes his way into the limelight, but allows others to shine? A perfectionist, who appreciates the fine arts? If you're in a romantic relationship with the Perfect type, you've formed a partnership with an extraordinary man. In fact, virtually all of the world's great artists, composers, philosophers, inventors, and theoreticians share this Personality type. The Bible is just bursting with men who demonstrate the characteristics of the Perfect man, including Jacob, Moses, Solomon, Elijah, Elisha, Jeremiah, Isaiah, Daniel, Ezekiel, Obadiah, Jonah, John the Baptist, and the apostles John and Thomas.[1] Quite a hall of fame, wouldn't you say?

The Perfect man is the second most obvious to spot in a crowd, but not because he's loud. Quite the contrary: he's very quiet. He speaks softly, because he doesn't want to draw attention to himself. He may even speak so softly that you have to ask him to repeat what he said. His clothing is quiet as well: he chooses low-key, traditional styles and colors like navy and gray. These are the men with twenty gray suits in the closet, and when you ask what they want for Christmas, they respond, "A gray suit." While the Popular man is open, the Perfect man is closed. He has a closed mouth, operating on a need-to-know basis. He won't tell you stories; he'll tell you the facts. His body language is also closed, with his hands held close to his sides and gestures kept to a minimum. And, finally, he has a closed life. Not only will he resist sharing intimate details of his life with strangers, he'll resist sharing intimate details of his life with his own wife or girlfriend.

Perfect Strengths

Extremely Organized

A surefire way to quickly determine whether or not your man fits this Personality is by looking at his personal space: his car, his office, his closet, and so forth. If it's neat and orderly, you're in a relationship with a Perfect type. Here's the quickest way: look at the garage. If it looks better than your living room, you know you're onto something. Just for fun, I've been wandering the neighborhood and peeking into garages every chance I get. The Perfect man's garage is often open because Mr. Perfect is in there putzing around. (See the next section to learn why!) I spotted one garage with wall-to-wall carpeting, beautifully framed pictures on the walls, and *curtains* on the windows! The screwdrivers and other hand tools were lined up in size order on a white pegboard. One side of the garage had white floor-to-ceiling storage cabinets, while the other two sides had elevated shelves for storing boxes. You can bet those boxes are neatly packed, labeled, and numbered, with a cross-reference system so he can immediately put his hands on any item in any of the fifty-seven boxes. There was even a washbasin so he could clean his hands before going back into the house.

If your man's garage is a wreck, he's probably a Peaceful man. The irony is that he may not have nearly as much stuff to store as most of his neighbors, but he will make absolutely no provision for storing what he does have. It's just thrown in heaps on the garage floor. He may occasionally feel very ashamed of this, but not ashamed enough to actually get up and do something about it. Which brings me to an important point: your man may be Perfect at work, but 100 percent Peaceful at home. His work office is no doubt neat and organized, but his home office is a catastrophe. The Perfect-Peaceful man returns home from work completely depleted of energy. He's the classic couch potato. He can't understand men who run giant corporations all day, then come home and play tennis. (Only Powerful men can do that!) If you've got a Perfect-Peaceful man in your life, I'll bet you've observed this seemingly conflicting pattern.

Practical

The Perfect man is the original Mr. Fix-It. One of my neighbors is an attorney, but I often see him in his perfect garage with his power tools making bookshelves and cabinets and such. This is the ideal person to have on hand come Christmas Eve or when you buy a new computer. In fact, any time instruction manuals rear their ugly heads, you'd better find yourself a Perfect man. He's the only one who will actually read them. He *likes* reading instruction manuals. My friend Joan told me that when they bought a new car, her husband sat down and read the entire owner's manual before anyone was allowed to drive the car.

This guy loves charts. When our neighbors Bob and Debbie brought their first child home from the hospital, Bob made a chart to keep track of the baby's every move, from number of hours sleeping and crying to the number of wet and messy diapers changed each day. Debbie reports that he has a giant whiteboard in their bedroom where he keeps track of their investments and liabilities and the progress they are making toward digging out of debt. Whenever they have to make a family decision, he breaks out his clipboard and makes a pros-and-cons chart.

The Perfect man keeps careful track of his business expenses, mileage, even grocery items he notices are out of stock, and anything else you can list or chart.

Self-Sacrificing

Many Perfect men are give-aholics. They'll work around the clock to provide the very best for their families—only the finest clothes, the finest schools, and so forth. They'll shower their wives with fine jewelry, presented while enjoying fine dining. They not only give sacrificially to their family but to friends, as well. I mentioned earlier that one of our neighbors, a Perfect type, owns a successful RV dealership. One day, out of the clear blue sky, his wife called to tell us he thought we might need a free vacation using one of his RVs. When we went to pick up the $150,000 vehicle, not only would he not accept a penny, he insisted on filling the gas tank. He has extended this gesture to many couples in the neighborhood.

When the church ran out of space for Sunday school, this man faithfully drove RVs to the church parking lot early Sunday morning and allowed them to be used as classrooms. When another friend faced a family crisis, he paid for a Christian counselor to help her work through it. In fact, whenever a need in the church or neighborhood arises, he is first in line with a donation and offer of assistance. He is just about the most self-sacrificing person I know.

In his book *Transformed Temperaments*, Dr. Tim LaHaye explains this tendency: "It seems easier for a [Perfect] person to see through the sham and the shallow material rewards this world offers and to rightly evaluate eternal things. I have observed that many missionaries going to the foreign field have a higher-than-average degree of [Perfect] personality. This characteristic accounts for the fact that many gifted missionaries are willing to renounce the pleasures and possessions of this life to serve Jesus Christ."[2]

Solid Christian

Once a Perfect man commits his life to Christ, he usually becomes a pillar of the church. Just as he studies other instruction manuals, he devotes himself to studying the ultimate instruction manual: the Bible. Our friend Jack became a Christian during his retirement years. We bought him a Bible, and when we saw him a week later, he had already read from Genesis to 2 Samuel. The Perfect man knows his Bible inside out; his theology is flawless. Before long, he'll be teaching adult Sunday school classes. He may even decide to attend seminary to deepen his understanding of God's Word or to become a pastor.

Perfect Weaknesses

Unwilling to Admit He Has Any Weaknesses

Can I let you in on the inner workings of writing a book? I was just breezing through this book, coming up with great stories (well, I hope you like them!) and typing a hundred words per minute. I was having lots of fun, and frankly, it was almost too easy. Then I got to this chapter on the Perfect man, and the whole thing fell apart. I haven't worked on the manuscript in weeks. Why? Because not one woman I know who is married to a Perfect man would talk to me about her husband.

Now maybe you can understand a wife not wanting to talk about her husband's weaknesses, but I couldn't even get these women to talk about their husbands' strengths. I was baffled. Then one woman explained it this way: "If I talk about my husband's strengths and say that he fits in this category, then it will be implied that he also has the weaknesses."

"So?" said I.

"So," said she, "he doesn't want to be associated in any way with weaknesses. He thinks he needs to be perfect and worries that anything less is not good enough."

"Oh," I responded, although I still couldn't quite relate. In my mind, we *all* have weaknesses, and it's no big deal. But then it began to register: to the Perfect type, weaknesses—in fact, anything less than perfection—are a very big deal. In fact, it's enough to get downright depressed about. Enough to make a guy resentful, revengeful, and withdrawn.

The fear of their husband someday stumbling upon this book *for women*, picking it up, and reading far enough to uncover a comment remotely linked to a negative characteristic they *might* have was enough to make these normally talkative women fall silent. Because of their perfectionistic tendencies, these men can be extremely difficult to live with. His suits *must* be ironed the one true way, then they must be hung in the closet the one true way. Breakfast, lunch, and dinner must be served the one true way, or his wife will be constantly reminded that she is not measuring up. The kids must always behave the one correct way, or they'll be constantly reminded that they aren't performing up to expectations. And on and on it goes. Perfect types think perfectionism should be listed in the strengths column. It certainly can be a strength. However, those who have to live with them know that when perfectionism is pushed to an extreme, as it frequently is, it belongs right here in the weaknesses column.

Pessimistic

"No" seems to be this man's favorite word. He's also a big fan of "No way." "That's impossible." "It'll never work." "What a dumb thing to say." "How on earth could you think that?" "Of all the crazy ideas." Well, you get the picture. For every brilliant suggestion you make, he's got a dozen reasons why it's actually a stupid suggestion. The eternal pessimist, he views the world through gray-colored glasses.

You started dating him because he was the strong, silent type. But now you realize, "Hey, that man doesn't talk to me." The deafening silence is not as romantic as it seemed in those old John Wayne movies. In real life, he's not quite so strong: in fact, he's the *sullen*, silent type. His dark moods seem to reveal a deep inner weakness masquerading as strength.

He dreams of having the perfect family and the perfect job. Then when life doesn't turn out perfectly or doesn't measure up to his ideal, he churns it around inside, becoming withdrawn, resentful, and increasingly pessimistic. Yet, when you ask him what's wrong, you always get the same reply: "Nothing." You can't help wondering, "Gee, if nothing's wrong, why does he have that miserable look on his face?" Since he is often in relationship with a Popular type, life for the woman in his life becomes neither perfect nor fun.

Critical

How would you like to live with a man who criticized everything you did? A man who made sure you knew nothing you ever did was quite good enough, never quite up to his standards. Pretty demoralizing, wouldn't you think?

If the Perfect man isn't careful, he can actually crush his wife's spirit with his constant criticism and drive for perfection. Interestingly enough, the Perfect man can dish it out, but he can't take it. He wants to criticize everyone else, but when you criticize him, he shuts down and drops out of sight. He can become, in short, an emotional bully.

Living with a Perfect man is like living with a film critic who thinks your entire life is a movie. Unfortunately, no one in his family *ever* rates "two thumbs up." Instead, all he does is criticize, criticize, criticize. As one woman noted, "He constantly criticizes my housekeeping, but he won't lift a finger himself. He just sits back and evaluates my work and points out everything I'm doing wrong."

After the honeymoon ends, women often realize that a Perfect guy can be extremely hard on his wife. Her housecleaning isn't good enough. Her child-rearing techniques aren't good enough. Her cooking isn't good enough. She doesn't spend money wisely enough. The list goes on and on. Day after day, on subject after subject, he makes sure his wife knows that she just doesn't measure up. In the same way these men keep track of the details on the job, they keep track of the details at home. They are especially adept at keeping track of everyone else's shortcomings.

Hypochondriac

As you can imagine, all this stored up resentment, bitterness, and anger can churn around inside the Perfect man and begin to take a toll on his health. Add to that his attention to detail, and you can end up with a man obsessed with the functioning of his body. He's constantly studying himself to see if anything's wrong. Under those circumstances, you can bet that plenty will go wrong. "Honey, can you look at this?" "Honey, I think I may be dying." It can really wear a woman down after a while—a very short while, I would imagine!

What Your Perfect Man Needs Most from You

By now, we all know your man's battle cry is, "Let's do it the right way." Although his most obvious need is to have everything done perfectly, he has some emotional needs you should recognize, as well. He needs a "sense of stability, space, silence, and sensitivity."[3] Let's look at each in turn.

Stability

The Perfect man's need for stability often shows itself in his passion for organization and schedules. He wants to see things done a certain way, at a certain time, every day. For him, that creates a stable life. You've probably noticed that his biggest thrill comes from analyzing something and then creating a system to make it run smoother. That's why he's constantly on a mission to get *you* organized. That's why he reorganizes the kitchen and types up index cards that show which shelf everything belongs on (or tries to persuade you that all would be well in the universe if only *you* would undertake such a project). Although it's hard to be treated like a project, try not to take it to heart. It's not that he doesn't love you, it's just that he craves stability. And a woman with a fly-by-the-seat-of-her-pants approach to life and household management makes him crazy.

Chances are, you crave the opposite. You crave change. And I'll bet you're even tempted to sneak up some change on that dear, dull man who always does things the same old way. Ho hum. Well, resist the temptation. He likes to do things the proven way. If you want a happy honey, try your best to create a stable environment for him to enjoy.

Space

Your man needs some space. He needs a place that is exclusively his. This may not be a problem during the dating phase of a relationship, when you and your man live in separate homes. But if you've married that Perfect man and now share a home, it's important for him to have a place that is strictly off-limits to you and any children you may have. Perhaps you have a small house and carving out such a place would be a great sacrifice.

Good.

Huh?

You heard me right. I said, "Good." That way, you'll have to think and plan and pray and work twice as hard as a woman with a great big house. When your husband sees you going above and beyond to meet his need for space, it will be that much more meaningful to him.

It may mean sacrificing your only storage closet. Or you may have to sew a fabric partition for the corner of your living room or bedroom. One option you might consider is buying an old cubicle from an office liquidator. Research local sources for used furniture, and you'll discover that there are huge warehouses filled with used office equipment. In addition to partitions of every style and color, they carry desks, swivel chairs, bookshelves, filing cabinets, you name it. Some of it will be in great condition; some not so great, but all dirt cheap.

Once he's got his own space, what's he going to do in there? Why, enjoy the silence, of course.

Silence

Generally speaking, most women are generally speaking. And generally speaking, it's driving the man in their life insane! Now, I know you love to talk, talk, talk. So do I. But if you're in a relationship with the Perfect guy, could you possibly give your honey one quiet evening a week? One night when you turn off all your electronic gadgets and refuse to make or take phone calls. (Sounds like blasphemy, doesn't it? What if someone is hit with a crisis? What if you suddenly remember you *had* a crisis and there's one woman left you haven't filled in on all the details?)

Silence means no television playing anywhere in the house. How about that? By the way, if you have more than one television, shame on you! Sell it and use the proceeds to finance your husband's quiet space. See how bossy I can be? I'll bet you're even having second thoughts about wishing I lived in your neighborhood.

Silence means no screaming kids. Put them to bed early or instruct them to play quietly in their rooms. If your kids can't quietly entertain themselves one evening per week, you've got a real problem on your hands.

Now, here's sacrilege, especially coming from me, a woman who serves on the board of advisors for a Christian radio station. Quiet may even mean no music—not even Christian music. Or your husband may enjoy quiet background music. Ask him.

Now you're thinking, *Oh, how dull! An evening with no TV, no phone calls, no screaming kids, and none of my fascinating stories.*

138

Think about this instead: Is it really so much to ask? One night out of seven to give your man the peace and quiet he truly needs? I don't think it is. Besides, you might just discover some unexpected blessings in the solitude.

You might consider making Sunday your quiet evening. It is the perfect day to rest and reflect, two things silence enables you to do more effectively. It's also the ideal time to plan for the week ahead so life runs more smoothly, which your man will surely appreciate.

Sensitivity

If there's one thing that absolutely drives your Perfect man crazy, it's insensitive, disorganized, forgetful, superficial, unpredictable people who can't show up on time. People like you, perchance? The reason these characteristics bother him so much is because of his deep need for stability. So realize that he's not picking on you (well, maybe he is, but . . .). It grates against the very fiber of his being when you waltz in an hour late with some story about running into the neighbor at the grocery store, and her brother-in-law's sister's cousin's nephew is graduating from Harvard. You just *couldn't* break away from a conversation of such importance to get home on time for his annual company Christmas dinner. The truth is (and he knows this full well), you completely forgot about the Christmas dinner. What's more, the only appropriate dress you own is either curled up in a heap on the closet floor or at the dry cleaner, where it's been since last year's Christmas party. Then you try to crack jokes and pretend, "Hey, it's no big deal."

The truth is, you were insensitive to your man and the things that matter to him. If you ever hope to achieve some of that perfect marital bliss you dream of, make every effort to give your guy the stability, space, silence, and sensitivity he yearns for. Lest you think I'm coming down too hard on you, I am well aware of just how cold and hurtful the Perfect Personality can be. But you've probably figured out by now that you can't change him, no matter how hard you try. If you're in a relationship or marriage with a Perfect man, you can pray for him, encourage him, and refuse to enable him, but you can't change him. What you can do, by the power of God, is accept him and learn to live with him, faults and all.

= 8 =

HE'S THE POWERFUL MAN

The Powerful man is a bundle of energy and enthusiasm, charging through life with grand schemes for changing the world and everybody in it. In fact, the quickest way to spot this Personality is to gauge the intensity of the air when he enters the room. (You can tell he's coming because the whole house shakes when he walks!) The minute he walks in, you know he's there. Now, if your relationship is positive, he'll bring excitement and electricity. If your relationship is in trouble, however, you may be having the most wonderful day of your life yet find yourself filled with stress as soon as he walks in the door. If your man's mere presence is enough to transform the atmosphere in a room, you're probably in a relationship with this Personality type.

Another way to spot this Personality is by his gestures. Does your man put his hands on his hips and lecture you? Does he pound his fist on the table to make a point? Does he point in your face? Is he the reason the phrase "in your face" was coined? This Personality type is the worst invader of personal space. He takes a step forward; you back up. He steps forward again; you back up. The next thing you know, you're cowering in a corner with his finger two inches from your nose!

If this sounds like your guy, read on.

Powerful Strengths

Born Leader

The Powerful man is a born leader. He's never bored, because he constantly dreams up new ideas, plans, goals, and ambitions. Not that he's a pie-in-the-sky idealist. Far from it. His feet are firmly rooted on terra firma. His sharp mind focuses its considerable intellectual prowess on the practical, rather than the theoretical.

There's not a company, organization, or church on the planet that he can't run with the utmost of confidence and skill. It doesn't matter if he has absolutely no idea what the organization does, he can rule it better than the bozos who are currently in charge. All the great crusaders against social injustice and most of the world's high-powered corporate and political leaders are, not surprisingly, this Personality type. If you study the lives of history's great generals and world rulers, you'll discover the same has been true from the beginning of human civilization. It's the Powerful types who shake things up and change the world in the process.

Chances are, your guy drives around in a big, fancy sedan or a flashy sports car. He has natural entrepreneurial tendencies and may well operate his own business. He might not run it for very long, though, because he quickly becomes bored and moves to another project. Researchers interviewed a panel of self-made millionaires looking for some trait they might have in common. They examined upbringing, education, and job experience and found nothing. Finally, they hit upon one common denominator: they each had started, on average, eighteen different businesses. While other men would be discouraged in the face of failure, the Powerful man's motto is "You haven't really failed unless you refuse to get back up." Now there's a classic Powerful line, don't you think?

Stan was a pillar in a church we once attended. One day, he came home early from work and announced that he had been fired. His wife wasn't too surprised. Powerful people get fired all the time because they don't hesitate to tell the boss what they really think. (And it's never anything complimentary—you can be sure of that!) Here's another hint: if your man has been fired from every job he's ever had because of conflicts with the boss, he's definitely a Powerful type! In Stan's case, he had told his boss in no uncertain terms that he knew a better way to run the business. Before firing him, the boss said something to the effect of, "Oh yeah? Try it." Dumb thing to say! Stan asked his wife if she would support him in the decision he had made on the drive home: to take their life savings (a few hundred dollars) and invest it in a business that would compete with his former employer.

She agreed.

Smart lady.

Within months, the business was turning a profit. Within a few years, he was a self-made millionaire. With the proceeds of the business, he almost single-handedly financed the construction of a gorgeous new church facility. He thought the old one was too dull and unworthy of God's glory; the new sanctuary is stunning—fit for a King, if you will! His take-charge style wasn't everyone's cup of tea, but he sure got the job done.

Decisive

As you can see from the above illustration, the Powerful man is extremely decisive. He's not one for making charts and endlessly analyzing data. He can't stand committee meetings or anything else he feels is a waste of his valuable time. His decisions are based on instinct, and he places great value on what his gut tells him. While others may dispute how he arrives at his decisions or try to "confuse him with the facts," the bottom line is he's almost always right. He does indeed have extraordinary instincts and an innate sense of what will work in any given situation.

I once had a boss like that when I worked for a computer manu- facturing company. He, too, was an entrepreneur and self-made millionaire. The engineering or accounting staff would agonize over data and present him with recommendations based on hours of careful analysis. He would listen for a few minutes, then rapidly pronounce his judgment. The employees would walk out mumbling about how it'd never work and how they "ran the numbers" or "tested the prototype." In the end, his decisions were almost invariably proven right.

Purposeful

Part of the reason the Powerful man enjoys so much success is that he lives with a constant sense of mission. He always keeps a clear purpose at the forefront of his mind and knows exactly what he wants to accomplish each day. He is not easily distracted like the Popular man. He doesn't make lists for lists' sake as the Perfect man does; he makes lists of things he intends to accomplish. And then he very quickly sets about getting them done. He doesn't waste time agonizing over minor details; once it's good enough to achieve his purpose, he moves on to the next conquest. And unlike the Peaceful man, he has an unlimited supply of energy.

Doer

Your man loves to "do"—especially to compete. The only potential problem is that he may push his children to win, win, win. (But we're not to his weaknesses yet, so let's look at the positive side of his competitive spirit!) Powerful men like to win, to be the best, and they want their family to be the best, too. Whether he's playing softball with the guys or Yahtzee with the kids, he likes to win.

The Powerful man will do more than watch his son play Little League—he'll coach the team. He'll do more than sit in the church pew—he'll take charge of the expansion program. (Powerful men absolutely *love* church expansion programs, because they can see tangible evidence of their actions.) Even on vacation, he wants to accomplish things, which can actually be a really neat quality if not taken to extremes. You won't find this man lounging around on a beach or relaxing on some boring cruise ship. No way! He craves adventure. He wants to take active, challenging vacations.

My friends David and Cindy take the most incredible vacations, thanks to David's determination to actively *do* something with his time off. They've taken a three-week hiking trip across New Zealand. They've traveled throughout Indonesia and Irian Jaya using every mode of transportation imaginable, from Jeeps to dugout canoes. The last I heard, they were planning an African safari. (As you've probably guessed, David is another of those self-made millionaires. He has to be in order to afford these lavish trips. Best of all, he doesn't have to plead with the boss for time off. He *is* the boss.)

What's really exciting, though, is that they've taken their children along on trips like llama trekking in Oregon and white-water rafting in Colorado. These kids would be bored stiff with something as tame as Disneyland, which I think is a very good sign.

Principled

Bob, a top sales executive for a local computer company, recently told me, "If you don't do the right thing and stand your ground, you could easily become corrupt in this business. I believe in telling the truth, no matter what, with no shades of gray. Whether it's good or bad, I tell it like it is. In the short run, maybe it has cost me a few sales, but over the long-term I know it will help me."

A few months ago, Bob was offered a huge promotion, which is usually irresistible to the ambitious Powerful man. The money would have been double his present salary, and the position would have brought incredible status. Accepting the position, however, would have meant uprooting his family, leaving his church and his friends. Bob said, "Forget it." His colleagues were shocked.

Powerful Weaknesses

Embarrassing Scenes

Linda loves her Powerful husband, but she says she's fed up with him constantly causing embarrassing scenes.

> We're not welcome at neighborhood parties anymore because of the way my husband always stirs up controversies. He thinks it's fun and flatters himself that he's getting the conversation going. But no one else enjoys it. We'll be in a group of twelve people, and Bob will be the only one talking for hours. Not just talking, though, stating his controversial opinions in a very argumentative tone of voice. I plead with him not to, but he can't seem to control himself.
>
> When we get home, I'll say something like, "You really ought to give other people a chance to talk once in a while." And he'll argue that no one else had anything to say. He doesn't realize the effect his behavior has on other people. I can tell by their faces they are so frustrated and fed up, they don't want to say anything for fear they might add fuel to the flame. I'm constantly embarrassed by his displays.

Demands Respect for His Rights

The Powerful man is big on his rights, and when he feels they haven't been respected, he's not afraid to speak up. He has a very short fuse! I think Linda's husband is a bit extreme, but I've met enough men like him to know he's not as uncommon as we might hope. She continues:

> The other thing he does is fight with sales clerks, waitresses, teachers, you name it. Whenever we go out, I'm always afraid it's going to end in conflict. More often than not, he sees "injustice" and he has to fight to make it right. The waitress took too long, so he'll fight with her and not leave a tip. Or

the food isn't hot enough, so he'll demand a discount. Or our flight will be delayed a half hour, so he'll put up a big stink with the stewardess and demand credit toward future flights. Sometimes he actually does get his money back or freebies, but it's hardly worth the hassle and humiliation.

No one is ever good enough for Bob. He thought our daughter's kindergarten teacher was incompetent, so he demanded that our daughter be put into a different class with the top teacher. Within a matter of weeks, he had a litany of complaints against the new teacher. He started hinting around that I should homeschool, but I have no doubt I wouldn't measure up, either.

Workaholic

Susan shared her frustration with her husband, Jim: "He spends all day in his home office, working around the clock. If he takes a break, he feels guilty, no matter how many hours he has put in. It's totally obvious to me that his work means more to him than I do. He's a giver of *things*, but I'm not a collector of things. I didn't marry him so I'd have someone to take charge of my business affairs; I married him to have and *to hold*."

Unfortunately, the Powerful type who aggressively pursues his wife before the wedding may want little to do with her after the wedding. He has conquered her and now is ready for new conquests. It's not unusual for him to turn to his work as a source of challenge, perhaps working sixty or more hours per week. He can turn into the absentee husband and father, bringing home lots of money, but very little of himself.

Project Not People Oriented

The Powerful man cares about projects, about what needs to be done, and in his mind, everything needs to be done right *now*. Susan gives an example.

My husband and I were put in charge of organizing our neighborhood's informal welcome wagon. It wasn't the world's most exciting organization, but they did a pretty good job. Well, within days of taking over the reins, Jim had this brilliant idea—from some seminar he'd attended at work—about giving everyone a sense of ownership. I guess in the solitude of his home office it seemed like a great idea. Without consulting me or anyone else in the group, he conjured up a grand vision and put together an elaborate plan of action to bring it about. Over the course of about a week, he called and recruited various individuals to fill new staff positions he had single-handedly created. Then he sent out a newsletter announcing the reorganization and revealing his personal selections for each of the newly created jobs. As you can imagine, people hit the roof! Especially the people who formerly controlled the group, whom he conveniently left out of his grand scheme. To this day, some of the neighbors still harbor hard feelings toward Jim. But in his mind, it was a project. He didn't stop to think about the people involved or how they might feel about the changes. He saw a problem, found a solution, and implemented it without consulting anyone else.

The Powerful man needs to allow people to give input on decisions that affect them and realize that, except in the case of extreme emergencies, nothing needs to be implemented right *now*.

Matter-of-Fact

The Powerful man doesn't care for small talk; he only wants to talk about important things. And of course, he alone is capable of determining which topics are important enough to justify his attention. Whether he's talking to an employee, his girlfriend, his wife, or his children, he wants to know, bottom line, what's the problem to be solved? He'll never sit and listen for the sake of listening. He listens so he can then tell you what to do to fix it. No matter how complex the problem, no matter how deep the emotional wound, his advice is the same: fix it and move on.

You may have noticed that he speaks in very short sentences, loaded with action words. And he doesn't like people who go off on tangents; he wants to stick to the issue at hand. He frequently interrupts others and finishes their sentences for them. Rather than actively listening, he'll be busy jumping in to offer a plan of action.

Susan reports that Jim never gives her an opportunity to talk about her feelings.

> He is emotionally unavailable. He doesn't want to get close to me, and he won't let me get close to him. When I had a miscarriage earlier this year, after six years of waiting for a baby, I desperately needed to talk about what I was going through. His attitude was, "Let's just forget about it. There's nothing we can do to change the situation, so what's the point of talking? Talking won't change anything." He just couldn't understand that talking was part of the healing process. It was very devastating for me.

The Powerful dad will rarely play with his children just for the sake of playing and spending time together. As always, he has to be accomplishing something. Susan reports, "Jim worked with the boys to build a tree fort, and that was great. But once the tree fort was finished, the boys wanted him to sit in it with them and goof off. Well, Jim wanted to conquer the next project. I think the boys were hurt; they had hoped the togetherness they enjoyed during the building process would continue. It didn't."

Defensive

As I mentioned when I introduced you to the Powerful woman, one popular book on Personality types actually lists this quality under the "strengths" category. But I think it's pretty obvious that this is a weakness. The Powerful man gets defensive easily. If you ask him a question, he views it as a challenge to his authority. Of course, if you're in a relationship with a Powerful type, you're probably a Personality that likes to ask tons of questions (Peaceful or Perfect).

You need to be particularly on guard in the area of child-rearing. If you're raising children with a Powerful husband, remind him that just because your children are asking questions doesn't mean they are defying him or challenging his authority. Children genuinely need clarification; they need to ask questions. If he closes the door to them, he will exasperate his children—something the Bible specifically warns fathers not to do.

What Your Powerful Man Needs Most from You

Your man storms through life announcing, "Let's do it my way." He loves to shake things up and make things happen. Which is great. Unless of course, it's *your* house he's shaking up. If you want to find contentment in your relationship to the Big Boss-Man, you would do well to keep in mind his deepest heartfelt needs. Now, I know what you're mumbling: "The guy doesn't have a heart." Yes, he does. And the best way for you to reach that heart is by feeding him the emotional food that he needs: a sense of obedience and an appreciation for his accomplishments.[1] Here are some suggestions to help you do just that:

Sense of Obedience

Just typing that word *obedience* gave me the heebie-jeebies. But, hey, remember the traditional marriage vows: "To love, honor, and o-o-o-o-bey." Well, this man actually expects you to follow through on that commitment. Imagine the nerve! Seriously, I know how bossy, domineering, and tyrannical these guys can be, but if you want your Powerful man to rest secure in your love, show him that you really are trying to obey (ouch, there's that awful word again). Proverbs 31:11 says, "Her husband has full confidence in her."

Here's how the Littauers put it in their book *Personality Puzzle*: the Powerful type likes people who "are supportive and submissive, see things their way, cooperate quickly, and let them take credit," and they dislike people who "are lazy and not interested in working constantly, who buck their authority, get independent, or aren't loyal."[2] Does that mean you should blindly follow wherever your Powerful boyfriend leads? Should you let a Powerful husband storm through life like the proverbial bull in a china shop, treating you, your children, and everyone else as nothing more than obstacles to his goals?

Definitely not. That's not good for any of you, least of all for him. You have a right to express your concerns and your viewpoint. You have a right to let your man know exactly where you stand and when he's standing on your toes. But once you've clearly communicated with him, try backing off and praying. There's power in prayer—put it to work for you. Pray daily that God will bring out the best in your Powerful man. He's God enough to do it! One thing's for sure, constant nagging won't do a bit of good and may, in fact, make your husband more intractable.

Now the upside of all this is that the guy is almost always right. Which, you protest, is actually one of his most annoying qualities. Nevertheless, the sooner you recognize that your man has extraordinary instincts and a natural flair for leadership, the easier it will become for you to follow his lead.

Appreciation for Accomplishments

Your Powerful man will come home with tales of how hard he's working and complaints about the long hours, the stress, the sacrifice, and so forth. And you'll be inclined to say something like, "Oh, honey, I wish you wouldn't work so hard." Wrong sentence, ladies. What he wants you to say is, "Wow! No one on earth can work as hard as you. You are amazing. I mean, you are a one-man working machine. What you can accomplish is unbelievable. I stand in awe of you."

Now I know you were just trying to encourage him when you told him to stop working so hard. But the reality is that he lives for accomplishments. Telling him to stop accomplishing is about as encouraging as telling a world-renowned pianist to stop performing. Besides, he doesn't want your advice. (If he wants your advice, he'll give it to you.) What he wants is recognition. If you're married to a Powerful man, he has a burning need to accomplish great things. This doesn't mean you sit in silence while your husband abandons the family in headlong pursuit of his projects. No. You ask him to meet you halfway. You sit down and hammer out a compromise everyone can live with. If he's unwilling to yield, you pray like crazy and refuse to enable him when his behavior is unhealthy or out of bounds.

If you have a Powerful man in your life, be thankful for all of his good qualities. Rather than fretting over his challenging characteristics, pray to the God who can change both of your hearts. I would strongly encourage you to read *The Power of a Praying Wife* by Stormie Omartian. I highly recommend this book to all wives, but it's a must-have for those of you who are married to (or plan to marry) a Powerful man.

=9=

HE'S THE PEACEFUL MAN

We've looked at the three other male Personality types in action, and if none of them sounded like your guy, he's probably the Peaceful type. And believe it or not, that's often the only way to identify this Personality: by process of elimination! The Popular type is extremely loud, the Perfect type is extremely organized; the Powerful type is extremely forceful, but the Peaceful type is not extremely anything. He has a chameleon-like ability to be all things to all people as the need arises. He has a dry wit and can be lots of fun like the Popular type. He enjoys routines, which may make him seem as organized as the Perfect type. He never gets into any conflict on the job, so he'll stay with the same company for twenty years and end up the head of a department. Actually, he can often fulfill the role of boss even better than the bossy Powerful type.

There are some visual clues to look for, chief of which is his casual appearance. This guy will almost always wear the most casual outfit possible for the occasion. He'd rather wear a two-piece than a three-piece suit. He'd rather wear slacks and a sports jacket than a suit. And he'd rather wear khaki shorts and a T-shirt than just about anything else in his wardrobe. His clothes are usually wrinkled. It doesn't matter how much starch his wife uses, his clothes will be a rumpled mess by the end of the day. That's because he lives by the motto "Why stand when you can sit? Why sit when you can lie down? And when sitting, sit as close to reclining as you possibly can!"

When a Peaceful husband comes home, his wife may not even notice for an hour or so! If she's working upstairs, he'll come in quietly and sit down on the couch. He may pick up a newspaper, but more likely, he'll pick up the channel surfer. But he won't holler, "Honey, I'm home." He'll patiently wait for her to come on down. If anything, his presence will have a calming effect on the atmosphere of the home.

Peaceful Strengths

Nice Guy

The Peaceful man is, without a doubt, the nicest man in town. I think Dr. Tim LaHaye sums up this man perfectly in his book *Transformed Temperaments*:

> The easiest people to get along with in life are Phlegmatics [Peaceful types]. Their calm, easygoing nature makes them well liked by others, and their clever wit and dry humor makes them a joy to have around. They qualify for the "Mr. Nice Guy" label wherever they go. In fact, Phlegmatics are usually such good people that they act more like Christians before their salvation than other Personality types afterward.[1]

Kids—and adults—find comfort and reassurance spending time with this steady, lovable man. He's nice to be around because he's always the same no matter what the circumstances. He's the same yesterday, today, and forever, even if the whole world seems to be falling apart. When you can't count on anything else, you can count on the Peaceful man to remain unchanged. This is in sharp contrast to the Popular man, whose mood is up one minute and down the next, or the Perfect man, who can slip into deep depressions, or the Powerful man, who might explode at the slightest provocation.

Great Listener

Peaceful men are great listeners, both at home and on the job. You see, all three of the other Personalities have to jump in when someone else is talking. The Popular man constantly interrupts because he thinks he has something funnier or more interesting to say. Or he wants to top your story with one of his own. The Perfect man wants to give you detailed advice on how to make everything right. The Powerful man wants to dish out some orders about what you need to do right now to take charge of the situation. Not the Peaceful man. He's content to sit quietly and listen.

When I worked in corporate America, I had a Peaceful co-worker named David who had a very sympathetic ear. People would come from all parts of the building to sit in his cubicle and tell him their tales of woe. We're talking about people he hardly even knew. Somehow, they found out that here was a man who took time to listen. And so a never-ending stream of people came, not to seek his brilliant advice or to receive a battle plan on how to make it right. They didn't even want someone to crack jokes and cheer them up. They wanted a listening ear.

On the home front, the wife of the Peaceful man often gets frustrated with him because he "wastes time" sitting around with the kids, doing nothing. Such wives would do well to take note of how, in the midst of all that "wasted" time, their husbands manage to find out what their children are really thinking and feeling.

Diplomatic

The Peaceful man believes everything should be done properly and with absolute dignity. He never, ever raises his voice in public. He is constantly mindful of everything he does and would rather die than draw attention to himself. He considers politeness a top priority and carefully weighs every word he speaks, for fear he might inadvertently offend someone. As you might guess, he is an extremely pleasant, enjoyable person to be around. And because of his inner drive to maintain peace and harmony in relationships, he has an extraordinary ability to mediate problems—whether sibling rivalry or warring nations. He also performs well under pressure, because he can almost always remain calm, even when everyone around him loses their cool. That's why many diplomats and high government officials have this Personality.

I think diplomacy even plays a role in his approach to the ice-cream shop. While the woman in his life spends twenty minutes trying to decide which of the 259 flavors she wants, the Peaceful man always orders the same flavor: vanilla. There's just something about the color white that seems to appeal to him. I guess it's an easygoing, noncontroversial color. No one's going to be offended. No one's feelings will get hurt if you order vanilla ice cream.

Steady

When it comes to his career, the Peaceful man is best described as competent and steady. He probably won't start his own business, but he makes a wonderful business partner. He also makes an excellent administrator because he is content to perform routine tasks day in and day out. Most school administrators (and many elementary school teachers) are this Personality.[2]

He's probably not going to become the next president of General Motors. Instead, he will be among the often-unsung heroes, the "Steady Eddies" who are the true backbone of every organization. He may not be loud like the Popular man, or detail oriented like the Perfect man. He may not shake things up like the Powerful man. But no company in the world could survive without these folks who quietly get the job done behind the scenes. He doesn't ask for credit or glory. He's a team player, liked and admired by his co-workers.

Solid Finisher

Although the Peaceful man is not one for launching big projects, he's definitely the man to have on hand when it comes to *finishing* a project. His specialty is persistence. A friend of mine, Denise, who has a solid understanding of her husband's Peaceful Personality type, has used her awareness of his "finishing" abilities to her advantage. She recalls one incident:

I remember when we first moved into our new home, and I wanted to make a bold design statement. You know, by painting the walls with bold colors. One day, when my husband was at work, I painted the dining room dark green. I mean a dark army green. Imagine my husband's surprise when he got home and heard me humming, "We're in the army now. We're in the army now!" Needless to say, he was not pleased.

You see, he wanted white walls. That's the way they had it in the model home. That's the way they were when we moved in. And, as far as he was concerned, that's the way they should stay. No need to launch a big project to change the status quo. Since the Peaceful man is a peacemaker by nature, he decided not to make too big of an issue about the green in our dining room *provided* (and the key word here is *provided*) I agreed to let the rest of the walls in the house stay white. I went along with it at first, but one day I got to thinking: "White walls? How dull. What kind of a statement do white walls make?" Then a brilliant idea struck me. I knew that if I went out and bought the paint and got the project started, he couldn't stand seeing it left undone.

So, guess what she did? She went out and bought purple paint (oh, don't gasp; it was a light purple!) and casually rolled a bit of it on each wall. Just enough to get the project underway. Then, when her husband returned home, he couldn't stand the lack of harmony in the walls, so he slowly, painstakingly finished the job. Well, shame on her for doing such a thing! It just goes to show that understanding the Personalities can be dangerous at times. Let me encourage you to resist the temptation to use your newfound knowledge to manipulate your unsuspecting boyfriend or husband.

A Man of Quiet Integrity

A Peaceful man probably won't make it to the top of the corporate ladder, no matter how insistently you urge him onward and upward. It's doubtful that he'll ever rake in a six-figure salary or win any awards. But chances are, he could go back to any company he has ever worked for and be warmly received. That's not to say the Peaceful man can't have a successful career. Former presidents Gerald Ford and George Bush are both Peaceful men who achieved tremendous success. They climbed to positions of power not by sheer force of their will or because of their charismatic personalities but because of their character.

What's more, the Peaceful type does not have any enemies; everyone likes him. While flashier men fizzle out and more brilliant men burn out, the Peaceful man remains steady. He stays loyal to the company and will rarely quit a job, no matter how unpleasant the situation becomes. If your man has been with the same company for many years, you can bet he has strong Peaceful tendencies.

One of my absolute favorite movies is *Chariots of Fire*, which tells the true story of British Olympic gold medalist Eric Liddell. The movie recounts Eric's steady progression toward the Olympic Games. He's not flashy. He's not driven to beat the competition. He simply knows that God has given him an extraordinary gift, and he wants to use it for God's glory. This is in sharp contrast to the other leading figure in the movie, a Powerful type, who prepares for the Games with a vengeance, bending the rules in a headlong rush to win at any cost. If you ever want to see a vivid portrayal of the contrast between God-confidence and self-confidence, the difference between one who is called and one who is driven, by all means, watch the movie. It's a fascinating character study.

Eric methodically prepared to compete in the 100-meter race. However, when he discovered that the race was to take place on Sunday, he refused to run. When the British Olympic Committee got word of this, they were furious with him. I mean, hey, they didn't know it was going to become an Academy Award–winning movie. All they saw was their great hope of glory dropping out of the race. They called a high-powered meeting with the Prince of Wales himself in attendance and tried to intimidate Eric into backing down from his principles. He was polite but completely unmoved. In his quiet, steady way he maintained his integrity.

Eric entered the 400-meter race (scheduled to be run on a different day), a race he was completely unprepared for and had no hope of winning. To everyone's astonishment, he won it anyway. He was a man of quiet integrity. What a picture of the incredible potential of the Peaceful Personality.

Cares for the Sick

My girlfriend Carol (a strong Powerful mom) had invited us for dinner one evening. We talked in the afternoon, and all systems were go. I was dressed and ready when the phone rang. Carol needed to cancel dinner. "Amy was asleep all afternoon and I figured, 'Hey, this is great. I can get lots done.' It never even occurred to me that something might be wrong with her. The minute Chris walked in, he put his hand on her forehead. Sure enough, she had a fever. Within minutes, he was wiping her head with a moist cloth and pumping her with fluids and medicine."

Now, if it were up to Carol, we would have gone ahead with our plans for the evening. But her husband is a Peaceful man, and there was no way he was going to neglect a sick child. I tried to talk her out of bringing dinner to us, and a battle of the Powerful moms was underway. She won. She came rushing over with hot lasagna, garlic rolls, and salad. We stood chatting for two hours (about how to get our kids under control, of course). Meanwhile, back at the ranch, Chris, aka Florence Nightingale, spent the evening caring for the sick.

Of course, the flip side is also true. Peaceful men enjoy being cared for when they are the sick ones . . . or even just the tired ones. I remember how much my Peaceful father enjoyed resting while we kids paraded into the room with warm washcloths to soak his forehead when he returned from long road trips.

Lifelong Friends

When you combine his loyalty, his knack for diplomacy, his subtle wit, and his aversion to conflict, it's not hard to understand why the Peaceful man keeps his friends for a lifetime. He's not big on huge parties and doesn't maintain a social calendar featuring a cast of thousands, though. Instead, he'll devote himself to a small band of friends: his golfing buddies, his fishing buddies, or in my father's case, his beer buddies. My dad had the same circle of friends from when he was a teenager until his death at the age of eighty-two. I can remember the same group of men gathering virtually every weekend to swap stories over beer and fat pretzels at the kitchen table, or to putter around the garage working on old cars.

Peaceful Weaknesses

Slow Moving

The wife of a Peaceful man is the most likely to hear comments about how lucky she is to be married to such a great guy. He's so sweet, so lovable, so patient. Who on earth wouldn't be thanking the heavens above for such a precious gem of a guy? His wife, that's who! Believe it or not, this easygoing man has some extremely annoying weaknesses. Chief among them is that he appears to have only three speeds—slow, unbelievably slow, and comatose. His co-workers don't see this side of the Peaceful man because typically he works hard on the job and tries to be friendly toward everyone. However, doing so completely drains him of energy. When he comes home, he has absolutely nothing left to give to his wife and children. He shifts into low gear and proceeds to drive his family nuts.

Speaking of driving, the surest way to spot a Peaceful man is on the road. He even *drives* slow.

Unmotivated

Some Peaceful men are not only slow, they are downright lazy. Now, I know that doesn't sound very nice, but it's true! They just can't seem to muster enough motivation to get anything accomplished. A woman will ask her husband to take out the trash, and he says, "Sure, honey." He's truly willing to get the job done; however, he lacks the motivation to get up off the couch and carry the bag to the curb. He has grand intentions about organizing the garage, but he can't muster the energy. He's been planning to repaint the house for years, but he can't marshal the strength. He'd like to plant a garden, but he's never been sufficiently inspired to till the soil. Perhaps if his wife starts the project, he'll get motivated to finish it. But not always!

Although most of these men will work steadily at their job, if they get laid off, they could be in for a serious problem. Why? Because they lack the motivation required for a successful job hunt. Or perhaps they have a job, but the pay is not sufficient to meet their family's needs or the job itself is unsatisfactory. They'll stick with it forever because they're not willing to put in the effort to make a change. (Please allow me to give a disclaimer here that not all Peaceful men are lazy. My father fit into this Personality, yet he was an extremely hardworking man. As you read about strengths and weaknesses throughout this book, please keep in mind that no one fits entirely into any of these Personality types. We're all unique!)

Indecisive

Sometimes the Peaceful man appears unmotivated when, in fact, he's merely indecisive. He doesn't like his job, but he can't decide if he dislikes it enough to move on. Besides, what if his new job turns out to be even worse? Fear—specifically the fear of making a wrong decision—is frequently the motivating force behind his inaction. So he makes up his mind not to make up his mind, which, ironically, is a very powerful decision.

TV Addict

Behold the quintessential couch potato. As one woman noted, "When my husband and I got married, he and the couch became one." When the Peaceful man gets home from work, he heads directly for the couch. Ideally, he'd like to have a tray permanently set up by "his" chair so he can eat dinner while watching TV. When the children try to talk to him, he mutters "huh" or waves them aside. His idea of a romantic evening together is asking his wife to sit down and watch TV with him. Within minutes, he'll be sound asleep. It's not unusual for a man with this Personality to spend most of his nonworking hours dozing in and out of consciousness, which makes him essentially an absentee father.

By the way, the ultimate gift you can give your Peaceful man is an easy chair. He'll love it! However, if you really love him, you may *not* want to buy him one, because he'll never be able to get back up again. And you don't want your guy stuck in an easy chair for the rest of his life, do you?

This will sound shocking to some, and I admit it's a radical step, but one woman actually hid the television from her husband. She said it was an act of sheer desperation. Every night after dinner, he would sit on the couch, click on the tube, and promptly fall asleep. Well, the kids needed daddy time, and she needed hubby time! She felt that the TV was a stumbling block preventing him from becoming the kind of man he wanted to become. (The Powerful wife always thinks she's helping when everyone else thinks she's being bossy and controlling.) At first he was in shock, but now he freely admits that his life is much better without that old TV monopolizing his time. He finally planted that garden he'd been planning, and he's even talking about organizing some of his paperwork. Would you take alcohol away from your alcoholic husband? Well, this wife removed her husband's addiction. Yes, he went through a period of withdrawal, but she reports that he's much better now!

Rain on the Parade

The Peaceful man is not big on generating new and exciting things for the family to do, which wouldn't be that big of a problem if it weren't for this particular character trait. Not only does the Peaceful man rarely instigate any new activities, but he'll rain on your parade when you try. "Sweetheart, let's go out to dinner, just the two of us." "I'm too tired," comes the reply. "Hey, honey, I've got a great idea! Let's have a family picnic this weekend!" A grunt in response. "Honey, what do you think?" A grunt in response. He may not come right out and tell you, "Forget about it, babe. Not gonna happen." He's too polite for that. But nine times out of ten, when time for the picnic rolls around, you won't be able to roll him out of bed. He'll just dig in his heels and refuse to go. "I don't feel like it" is all the explanation you'll get.

One woman exclaimed, after years of searching for common interests with her husband, "How can you cultivate common interests with someone who isn't interested in anything?" It's very hard, indeed. And without common interests, your marriage may also be very hard indeed.

What Your Peaceful Man Needs Most from You

If your man has a Peaceful personality, you're very blessed with someone who is almost always there to meet your needs. However, don't lose sight of the fact that he, too, has emotional needs. Consider the following.

Peace

His primary motivation in life is to avoid conflict, to live in harmony with himself and those around him. When a Peaceful husband comes home at the end of the day, the worst possible scenario is for him to walk into chaos—kids screaming, the kitchen torn apart, a wife who's ready to kill someone, *anyone*. If this is what your husband comes home to, don't be surprised when he immediately retreats to the couch and his beloved television set. Don't be surprised if he promptly falls asleep. That's his way of escaping the madness. I know how difficult it is when the entire world's gone mad and life is racing at breakneck speed, but do your best to make your home a refuge from the storm.

If you are married to a Peaceful husband, here are a couple of ideas that may help promote peace for your honey. First, use your Crock-Pot! Sounds crazy, I know. But the beauty of it is that you make the mess in the morning and have some peace and quiet before dinnertime. You might also invest in a variety of relaxing CDs, such as those that capture the sounds of nature—a waterfall, a gentle ocean, chirping birds. Well, you know the ones I'm referring to! Depending on your husband's personal taste, you might start a collection of classical music and instrumental hymns and praise music. (Chances are, he doesn't care for the lively praise and worship music; not peaceful enough!) If you're a stay-at-home mom with a baby, if you can rearrange her nap schedule so she's napping when Daddy gets home, that's a real bonus that enables you to have dinner in peace. Dad can have time with the baby after he's had a chance to relax. As an extra measure of peace, light some candles on the kitchen table.

One of the most significant things you can do to maintain the peace is to provide your guy with early warnings. That's because he requires plenty of advance notice about any upcoming events. If there is one thing he simply cannot stand, it's a sudden change of plans. He had his heart set on sitting and watching TV, and suddenly you spring a dinner party at the Joneses on him. Since he's generally slow to warm up to an idea, he needs to prepare himself ahead of time. If you want to get this normally mild-mannered man's blood boiling, just try sneaking something up on him without warning. *Look out!*

Again, my friend Denise shares an example:

One Wednesday evening my sister called to invite us to a birthday party for my niece. I hung up the phone, turned to my husband, and told him about the invitation. He hit the roof! I couldn't understand why he was so furious, but that didn't stop me from joining the battle. We argued vehemently for nearly forty-five minutes, when finally in exasperation I exclaimed, "What exactly is it that you have to do this Saturday that's soooo important that you can't attend my niece's birthday party?" Suddenly, he was quiet. "You mean it's on Saturday?" "Yes," I replied. "Oh, I thought you meant it was tonight. Sure, no problem. Of course we can go."

Denise reports with that, they both broke into hysterics and literally rolled on the floor with laughter. He had his early warning. Peace was restored to their household.

Relaxation

You may label your man lazy, but his emotional need for relaxation is as legitimate as any other emotional need, and it goes deep within his Peaceful personality. If you divorce him from his beloved TV (even if it means having his channel surfer surgically removed from his hand), it's up to you to replace it with something else.

How about a relaxing evening with you? Why not play some soft music? Perhaps a leisurely walk around the block? Be creative, and ask God to help you develop some positive alternatives.

Praise

Now this is the key that can really turn around your relationship with a Peaceful guy. Start noticing his many fine qualities, and begin expressing sincere praise and honest appreciation for them. As you do, don't be surprised if you suddenly discover that your boyfriend or husband develops "full confidence" in you (Prov. 31:11). He will begin to rest more securely in your relationship. You're probably thinking, *If I start being nice to him, he'll see right through that old trick. If I start praising him, he'll get suspicious and accuse me of being insincere.* If he's half Perfect, you may be right. He may react that way. Then you'll just have to work doubly hard to ensure that you are sincerely praising him, not just flattering him. There is a difference. Flattery is superficial. Praise takes the time to really *look* for the good and genuinely cherish it. Here's how the Bible puts it (with my slight modification): "Finally, wives of Peaceful men, whatever is true, whatever is noble, whatever is right . . . if anything is praiseworthy—think about such things" (Phil. 4:8).

Self-Worth

Your guy needs you to reassure him that he's a valuable human being even if he never accomplishes anything of great value according to the world's standards. It's quite likely that your easygoing man will never achieve the sort of success the world applauds. That's why he so much needs *you* to applaud him. That's why he needs you to build his self-worth with loving reassurance, instead of criticizing and belittling him. The ideal theme song for this guy is "The Measure of a Man" performed by 4Him. It points out that a man's physical appearance, the amount of money he makes, and the number of brilliant thoughts he may have do not really indicate what kind of man he is. One line in particular may prove especially meaningful to your Peaceful guy, as you assure him that you firmly believe it: "What's in the heart defines the measure of a man."[3]

Frequently remind your man of his many wonderful qualities: that people love him, that he's honest, hardworking, and loyal. Who needs flash when you can have substance?

I just want to encourage those of you who are married to a Peaceful man to ask God to help you *really believe* in your husband. Superficial words of praise are not enough. But as you come to genuinely believe in him, he will come to believe in himself. I often tell people who want to start their own business, "Believe in you and others will, too." Help your husband to believe in himself and other people will believe in him, too!

Loving Motivation

It goes without saying that you shouldn't nag your husband or boyfriend. Well, at least I hope it does. Solomon said it was better to live on a rooftop than with a nagging woman, and he was right. If nagging and goading could get the job done, believe me, ladies, chances are your man would have climbed Mount Everest and been the president of an international corporation by now. However, a Peaceful husband does require "loving motivation." Now, let's admit there's a fine line between nagging and loving motivation—and most wives haven't figured it all out yet.

Here's an example that may shed some light on the difference. Sarah's husband has an extraordinary talent for the guitar. However, he hadn't played in years. When they began attending a new church, the music program . . . well, it left a little to be desired, to put it mildly. By the pastor's own admission, it was a weak link in an otherwise growing, dynamic church. Sarah felt certain that if her husband broke out his guitar, he could make a huge difference in the quality of the church's worship experience. She suggested it. She suggested it some more. She mentioned it a few more times. *Years* passed, with her weekly nagging sessions going unheeded. Finally she shut up. About three years after they began attending, Sarah took her husband by the hand and walked over to the music director and declared, "This man is the most incredible guitar player you'll ever hear. If you don't recruit him, you're crazy." Then she turned around and walked away. The music director handled it from there, and Sarah reports that her husband has been blessing the congregation with his talent ever since.

Loving motivation works! Try it with your honey and see.

Part Three

UNDERSTAND YOUR RELATIONSHIP

How the Popular Woman Entertains (and Annoys) Her Man

Popular Woman + Popular Man

When two people who love the limelight get together, intense rivalry can result. Since both want to be the center of attention all the time, petty jealousy might develop if one starts to outshine the other. On the bright side, neither of you is inclined to hold a grudge, but if this issue constantly surfaces, there will be ongoing turmoil. One possible solution, of course, is to actively divide the glow. For example, one might shine in the area of the home and relationships, while the other shines on the job. Provided both are content with this scenario—that is, they get enough attention, approval, and affection—there shouldn't be an inordinate amount of conflict in this relationship.

When the Popular woman marries a Popular man, this combination becomes a very fun-loving couple who genuinely enjoy their life together. They no doubt have many friends and love throwing parties. Their children look forward to coming home (even though the house is a wreck), and their friends all wish their parents were just like the two of you.

If you are a Popular woman and you've married—or plan to marry—a Popular guy, you two will be great together when life is great. But when tough times inevitably come, you may lack the internal fortitude to see your way through. In particular, be on guard against financial setbacks. Neither of you may handle money well, so credit cards might be like a deadly weapon in your marriage. When you're having fun, you spend money. When you have a fight, you spend money. When you're worn out from a tough day on the job, you go out to dinner and spend money. Hopefully, one partner will land a sales job and make enough money to cover your cozy lifestyle. If not, you can expect money problems to be a significant issue throughout your lifetime, particularly in your retirement years.

Popular Woman + Perfect Man

Here's an extremely common combination and one that's fraught with heartache if not handled properly. Unfortunately, there are a great many things about the Popular woman that genuinely bother the Perfect man. For example, a Popular woman is often disorganized and inaccurate, two of the worst crimes imaginable to the Perfect type. Once married, the Perfect man starts to think his wife is just a show-off and soon grows impatient with her tendency to exaggerate and invent wild stories. It's equally hard on her because she's inclined to think, *How did I manage to marry the* one person *in the world who doesn't think I'm adorable?*

The Perfect husband enjoys people who are serious, intellectual, and deep, which often leaves his wife wondering why on earth he married a Popular type like her. However, if she wants him to be happy, she should try to have a sensible conversation with him . . . at least once a week.

This couple frequently gets into conflict over money management. One wife reported taking radical steps to eliminate the battle over money:

The first thing I did was get rid of all my credit cards. I mean, I just had to admit I couldn't handle the responsibility. The so-called convenience wasn't worth driving my husband nuts over. We used to share a checkbook, but it made him crazy. I'd write out checks or make withdrawals and not tell him about it. Then he'd go to balance the checkbook and find all these withdrawals that I was too embarrassed to tell him about. We fought about it all the time.

So then he got me my own checking account and gave me a set amount of money each month that I was in charge of. Well, I'd spend all the money in the beginning of the month, but then I was too embarrassed to ask him for more money, so I would bounce checks all over the place. Eventually, I just said to him, "I can't handle a checking account. I want a cash allowance." Now I have no access to credit cards or checking accounts. He gives me cash for groceries, gas, and household stuff. It sounds crazy, but it's made a big difference in our marriage. Now I don't give him all that grief. My spending is controlled because I only get a certain amount of cash to spend. I do my best not to ask him for more.

If my husband had come up with the idea, I probably would have been mad at him. But I'm the one who chose it. My spending was creating too much stress. I had to admit I have no self-control. I've tried many ways and none of them worked. For me, this is easier.

Well, I warned you that she took radical steps. Your situation may not be that severe. Nevertheless, if you and your Perfect husband engage in constant warfare over money, you might consider some radical steps of your own.

Another battleground for the Popular wife and the Perfect husband is the house. Specifically, his desire for the perfect home coupled with her inability to get it together. This combination obviously leads to major frustration on both sides. Believe me, I sympathize with your side of this battle. Nevertheless, I would strongly encourage you to take some action here. If you can possibly afford it, you might consider hiring a housecleaner to come once a week or even once a month. It may be well worth the expense if it keeps the peace. I have often hired housecleaners when involved with a demanding project; you don't have to make a lifetime commitment! Even if they only come once or twice, it might be just enough to get you headed in the right direction.

If you've got more time than money, buy some books on organization, and get excited about it. The internet is filled with websites, blogs, and ezines on personal and household management. Find a few that interest you and run with new ideas. With the right attitude, it really can be fun. Yes, fun! I'll bet you have some Perfect friends who would be willing to help you organize your home. Ask for their help. Even if you don't feel like it, do it for your husband's peace of mind.

As you may recall, the Perfect Personality has a heartfelt need for space. When I was a little girl, I shared a bed with my sister, Helen. We drew an invisible line down the middle, and if I dared to cross over, she'd whack me over the head. Naturally, I gave her the same treatment. The wife of the Perfect husband often feels like a little girl who just put her toe over the invisible line.

Before John and Debra moved into their dream home, John worked closely with the architect on the design for his ideal home office. It was going to be his hideout, his haven of rest. Debra reports how well it worked out.

He was so excited to put his desk in there. But soon after he moved in, I took it over. My papers were all over it at all times. The kids' toys were thrown everywhere, and the kids were in and out. And he was really uptight. He suggested I get my own desk and put it at the other end of the office. He still wasn't happy, because my desk was piled a foot high. It wasn't a big deal to me, but it really bothered him. Even when I clean it, it never looks as good as his. They are neat piles in my mind, but in his mind, they are still piles. When we began to talk openly about it, I also discovered he was really offended that I didn't keep the kids out of there, out of his space.

The Popular wife's Day of Fun can often turn into the Perfect husband's Night of Depression. Barbara recalls one such occasion:

I've always got a house full of kids. Well, on this particular day, I had a bunch of the neighbors' kids running around the backyard all afternoon. It had been raining for days, so they were covered in mud. To top it all off, we'd just bought a puppy, and he was traipsing mud all over the house.

I decided to bring the kids in the house, because they were destroying the backyard. They quickly got bored so we decided to make cookies. Needless to say, they got cookie dough and sprinkles all over the place. We were having a great time. I figured I had plenty of time to get the house in order before my husband came home. Then all of a sudden, my husband pulled into the driveway. I knew he was going to be upset, so I met him at the door and said, "Will you please leave? You can't come in right now." He said he just needed to grab something from his office, but before he could make it into the den, the baby came running out of the back room with frosting all over his face. My husband took one look at the backyard and the kitchen and went into shock. In my mind, it was a really fun afternoon; in his mind, it was completely unacceptable. He was very depressed that night.

Barbara also reports several occasions when her husband called home from work to ask, "How is the house doing?" "I couldn't believe it," she says. "He didn't ask how are *you* doing; he wanted to know if the house was okay. How are you performing? Are you keeping up? I was very hurt. He wasn't interested in me; he was interested in the house."

The Popular wife resents the Perfect husband's pessimism, while he thinks her optimism is foolish and shallow. The truth is, she *is* a poor judge of character and may run with the wrong crowd or misread the intentions of male friends. She may also send out the wrong message in the name of being friendly. When her perceptive husband tries to warn her, she attacks him verbally rather than heeding his wisdom.

If you're a Popular girl in a relationship with a Perfect guy, you two can learn a lot from each other, forming two halves of a wonderful whole, if you can get past your differences. Since you're the one reading this book—you're the one with the tools in your hands. I encourage you to take the first step.

Popular Woman + Powerful Man

These two actually make a fairly harmonious couple, provided she keeps the social wheels turning at a fast enough clip while he conquers the business world. Because they are both extroverts with an abundance of energy, they'll enjoy staying active together. Pity the poor little Peaceful child born to this pair!

When a Popular woman marries a Powerful man, conflict can arise if the husband views his wife as capricious and accuses her of getting nothing accomplished. She may not be goal oriented enough for his taste. He may also feel she spends too much time talking, especially talking on the phone all day long. He wants to see results, not relationships. To ease this conflict, the Popular wife should emphasize the results she has achieved through forming key relationships in the church and community.

If the Powerful husband's secondary trait is Perfect, then his Popular wife may discover another set of problems. After functioning in his extroverted Powerful mode all day at the office, he'll want to shift into his introverted Perfect mode in the evening. If the Popular mom has been at home all day without adult conversation, she'll be desperate for someone to talk to. Even when he's in high gear, the Powerful husband keeps communication succinct. He doesn't have the time or patience for long, involved stories; he wants people to get to the point. His natural tendency to become impatient with his wife's stories will be greatly magnified if his secondary trait is the Perfect type who views his home as a haven of rest, silence, and solitude.

If she chooses to marry a Powerful-Perfect man, the Popular woman should actively cultivate friendships with women, so that she has her share of adult conversation before her husband returns from work in the evening. She might also plan to go out one evening every week after getting the children off to bed. This will enable her to socialize, while giving her husband at least one quiet night in the midst of each hectic week.

Popular Woman + Peaceful Man

The Popular woman is almost always talking, talking, talking, loudly, loudly, *loudly*. In the beginning, her Peaceful boyfriend thinks it's cute. He may even marry her because he enjoys having someone who can make conversation. But after the honeymoon wears off, it becomes ridiculous. Doesn't she ever come up for air? Her incessant urge to make noise annoys her more reserved partner to distraction. He needs an opportunity to sit and work quietly, whether it's working on a crossword puzzle or paying the family bills. If his Popular wife fails to give him some time and space, he'll end up exhausted.

The Popular girl loves nonstop activities, but if she expects her Peaceful man to keep pace with her, she's in for a big surprise. If she demands that he keep pace with her, he will become sick with exhaustion. Larry and Susan are a case in point. Thanks to Susan, they had something going nearly every night of the week. All good things, of course. Monday night, missions society. Tuesday night, small group Bible study. Wednesday night, prayer meeting. Friday night, youth group fun night. (She volunteered them to lead the youth group.) Saturday, household chores and extra activities with the youth group. Sunday, church in the morning *and* the evening—with dinner guests in between. When Larry would beg Susan to slow down, she would accuse him of being unspiritual. She just couldn't understand what was wrong with that man. Where was his zeal for the Lord?

However, when she measured her spirituality as God does, not in terms of outward activity but inward fruit of the Spirit, Susan had to admit that her husband was far ahead of her. She may have been the chairperson of everything from the casserole committee to the missions society, but Larry was the one quietly cultivating a heart of love, joy, peace, patience, kindness, and self-control.

Another reason the Peaceful man may not want to follow along with a Popular woman's whirlwind schedule is because, quite frankly, she embarrasses him. He wants to be quiet and not make a scene. She actively tries to draw a crowd. She constantly overpowers and overshadows her man. Eventually he may resent her for it. She might also push and prod him along, thinking he moves too slowly, which again can yield resentment. She tosses out words without thinking, and he takes everything to heart, creating yet another breeding ground for resentment.

Warning to the Popular woman: if you marry a Peaceful man, your husband is the most prone to bitterness and resentment. Too many Popular wives are adored by absolutely everyone . . . except their own husbands. I don't want that to happen to you! You have so many wonderful qualities to offer to any man, regardless of his Personality. Prayerfully consider the suggestions in this chapter, and seek to adapt your personal style so you can live in harmony with your partner.

HOW THE PERFECT WOMAN DRIVES HER HONEY CRAZY

Perfect Woman + Popular Man

In the individual chapters on the Perfect woman and the Popular man, we warned that the Perfect wife tends to drive people away while the Popular husband, with his flexible conscience, tends to wander. Now I am not saying *all couples* with this Personality combination will end up a divorce statistic. However, based on years of dealing with women in bruised or broken marriages, I've concluded that this couple is the most prone to infidelity. As the eternal optimist, a Popular man will become frustrated by a Perfect woman's pessimistic attitude. His free-spirited nature gets crushed under the weight of her constant demands for perfection.

I met Barb, a trim, attractive woman in her late forties, at a women's retreat in Kentucky. Her husband of twenty years had just left her, and she was reeling in shock. Barb was the church secretary who did a perfect job running everything behind the scenes. Their weekly church bulletin was a thing of beauty with never a mistake in it. She even sang perfectly in the choir. Her home was perfectly decorated. In fact, it was the envy of the neighborhood.

Even though her husband didn't make much money, with her knack for bargain-hunting and dollar-stretching (not to mention her exquisite taste), she managed to transform it into something off the pages of *House Beautiful* magazine. But she wasn't some shallow, superficial woman. Far from it. She was often sought out by women in the congregation who admired her grasp of the Scriptures and the depth of her spiritual insight.

Everything was perfect. So why did her husband leave her? He found a less-than-perfect woman who accepted less than perfection from him. Was he right to do so? Certainly not; there's absolutely no excuse for his infidelity. We're not letting him off the hook here. He made the wrong choice. He committed a serious sin, one of the Big Ten. If our goal in this book were to find fault, this would be a no-brainer. We'd label him a jerk and be done with it. But our goal is to equip you to make the most of your relationship. And if that's your objective, forget about who's right and who's wrong, and pray that God will soften your heart and make you a more accepting person.

If you are a Perfect woman in a romantic relationship with a Popular man, don't despair. There is hope for this personality combination! This couple can have the most wonderful, passionate marriage if they savor the differences. My friend Cheryl, a Perfect type married to a Popular husband for thirteen years, shared the following story:

> My husband loves to tell stories, a quality I found attractive and engaging when we first met. I'm shy and soft-spoken, so I admired his ability to spin a yarn and hold an audience. After we were married, however, I came to realize how much of his storytelling was fictionalized, and I took it upon myself to correct his every embellishment. One day my dad took me aside and reminded me that it would be okay, in fact it might promote marital harmony, if I let Mike go on with his stories and not try to correct every detail. I agreed to try and was presented my first challenge at dinner that night.

We were out with two other couples and we started talking about the food at the Minnesota State Fair. A favorite of everyone there was the deep-fried cheese curds. Mike and I had talked about making them at home, but hadn't actually made them yet. But since that wouldn't be a very good story, he started telling everyone how we made them all the time.

"Oh, they're great," he said. "We just get out the deep fryer and cook 'em up."

With my dad's words ringing in my ears, I just nodded and smiled. I was becoming part of this conspiracy. I was letting my husband get away with this story. He couldn't believe it! He became even bolder. "In fact, we just made them last night. We took them with us to a potluck dinner, and our deep-fried cheese curds were the hit of the whole dinner!"

Wow, now everyone wanted to make deep-fried cheese curds at home, too. "You just use a deep fryer?" they asked. "Where do you buy the cheese curds?"

Mike was in his element until this question: "How do you make the batter?"

Ha! I thought. I knew he didn't have a clue about cooking. *Let's see you get out of this one, Mr. Smarty Pants.* I looked over at Mike with a grin. But he just turned to me and said, "How *do* you make that batter, Cheryl?"

Cheryl reports that she and her husband are blissfully happy in their marriage . . . most of the time, and that understanding the Personalities has gone a long way toward promoting harmony. I should point out that we're not overlooking the fact that her husband clearly crossed the line past embellishment with this particular story. If your husband embellishes to the point of falsehood, pray for him and privately "speak the truth in love." Cheryl, however, was absolutely right to resist the temptation to correct her man in public.

Perfect Woman + Perfect Man

These two perfect people should be perfect together, shouldn't they? Any problems? Just one: heaven help their children! In terms of their romantic relationship, they may spend so much time analyzing one another that they never take time to enjoy life. Since both are prone to depression, theirs can become a dark, brooding marriage after they say "I do." One partner is likely to be Perfect-Powerful while the other is Perfect-Peaceful. As has been mentioned, the Perfect-Powerful combination is perhaps the most difficult Personality to live with. Not only do they want everything done perfectly, they want it done their way *now*. The Perfect-Powerful partner's high-energy demands for instant action and total obedience can crush the life out of the Perfect-Peaceful partner, who is a low-energy, pure introvert. When the Peaceful tendency toward resentment joins forces with the Perfect tendency to hold permanent grudges, you can imagine the strength of the bitter root that might take hold. This is the couple who can live together in absolute silence for fifty years.

The best insurance for these two deep individuals is to actively maintain the romantic side of their marriage; both are incurable romantics. And love covers over a multitude of sins. So if you're a Perfect woman and God's blessed you with a Perfect man, don't let your relationship grow cold: look for creative ways to keep the romantic sparks burning and you can enjoy many happy years together.

Perfect Woman + Powerful Man

His battle cry is "My mind is made up; don't bore me with the facts." And of course, the Perfect wife is president of the International Bore People with the Facts Society. She is extremely detail oriented and cautious and will no doubt try to slow down her fast-action partner. Naturally, he has no interest in slowing down.

Anne and her husband, Jack, decided to buy a new house, so she spent weeks putting together a scrapbook of clippings of the ideal house: a page for each bedroom, two pages of kitchen features, and so forth. She then typed up a chart listing the exterior and interior features they were looking for along with a rating system ranking the importance of each feature. Then, as they looked at each house, she could complete the form, tally the results, and make a logical decision based on the facts.

House number 1 had a brick exterior, worth 10 points on a scale of 1 to 10. Since exterior sturdiness and durability were of extreme importance, that particular category carried a weight of 5 (10 × 5, or 50 points). She then rated each of the 20 features on the list (living room, fireplace, carpet condition, and so forth) and gave the house a total rating of 650 points. She did that for the next three houses, with ratings of 725, 350, and 450.

"Not bad for the first day of looking," she said to herself, knowing it would take many months to find their ideal home rated at 1,000 points. When they got back to the Realtor's office after their tour of homes, her husband dropped a bombshell. To her utter astonishment, he suddenly turned to the Realtor and said, "We'll take house number three." (Isn't it amazing that he didn't even consult his wife before making this declaration? Lest you assume he's just an awful guy, he later told her that it never even occurred to him that she *wouldn't* want to live in such an idyllic spot!) Well, she looked at her chart and realized it had the lowest rating. Before she knew it, her husband was putting in a formal written offer on the house. He liked the backyard with the stream running through it. He didn't care that the bedrooms were small, the carpet was shot, and the kitchen appliances were outdated. He had always dreamed of having a stream in his backyard.

Anne tried to reason with him by showing him the charts. She had the proof, but she could tell he wasn't listening to a word she said. While they were sitting at the Realtor's desk debating the merits of the house, another couple called to say they were ready to make an offer. The Realtor turned to Anne and Jack. It was the moment of truth. Would they trust the Perfect wife's flawlessly conceived and executed chart or the Powerful husband's childhood dream?

What would you do?

They followed the dream! They knocked down walls to expand the bedrooms, replaced the carpets, and installed new appliances. The one thing they couldn't have done was run a small stream through the backyard. As it turned out, that stream—complete with minnows and tadpoles—has been a continual source of joy for their family for the past fifteen years.

There's a time for analysis and a time for action. A time for checklists and a time to follow your heart. If you've got a Powerful honey, learn to trust his instincts. No, he can't always tell you exactly why, can't always provide chart-and-graph proof to support his case, but he has an uncanny ability to be *right*.

On the downside, he has an uncanny ability to run roughshod over your feelings. He doesn't like in-depth conversation or details. He's a big-picture person who likes to cut right to the chase. So if you're a Perfect woman in a relationship with a Powerful man, express your viewpoint clearly, as Anne did in the above illustration, and don't allow him to turn into a total bully.

Perfect Woman + Peaceful Man

She wants everything to be perfect, but perfect takes a lot of work. That's a problem right there, because the Peaceful husband isn't that big on work. He would rather kick back in his recliner than spend his weekends perfecting the house and keeping up with her endless checklists and charts filled with work. When he does complete her latest project, it's never quite up to her standards. She'll make him do it over and over and over again until it's done *right*—anything less than sheer perfection is never right in her book. He views her as too critical and judgmental. Since he can never please her anyway, eventually he figures, "Why bother?"

After the Perfect and Popular couple combination, I believe this pair is the second most likely to end in divorce. In this case, the Perfect wife's demands for perfection leave the husband feeling inadequate and emotionally drained. When he finally musters the strength to leave (and it usually takes many, many years) those outside the marriage will think: here was a man with the perfect wife—the perfect hairstyle, the perfect house, the perfect cook, the perfect everything. What more could he want? It's not that he wanted *more*; he wanted *less*. He wanted fewer demands for perfection and fewer feelings of never measuring up to her high standards. In many cases, he will find another woman who will accept him as he is rather than constantly demand perfection.

Here again, we're not saying the Perfect woman is an awful, no-good person whose Peaceful husband will be an innocent bystander with no choice but to run off. No doubt his sluggish, cavalier attitude may torment her for years. And no doubt his indifference can leave her feeling compelled to pick up the slack, carrying far more than her share of the load with the house and the children. As usual, there's enough blame to go around. But why settle for blame when you can have the joy of a happy marriage? See if using your newly found tools doesn't make a huge difference in your relationship. That will be far more productive and gratifying than sifting through the wreckage, looking for evidence to prove you were right and he was wrong.

12

How the Powerful Woman Lords It Over Her Man

Powerful Woman + Popular Man

As the newlywed glow fades, the Popular husband often starts to feel like being married to a Powerful wife isn't very much fun. He wants to have a good time, but she's bossing him around and giving him work to do. She also makes decisions without consulting him, which may or may not bug him. If he realizes that abdicating decision-making authority makes his life more fun, he may try to coast through the marriage and let her handle everything. That will work short-term, but will gradually erode their relationship.

Jane decided she'd pulled the wagon long enough for her "party boy" husband, Eric. One of the few places he'd agreed to help in the home was in taking out the garbage. However, when the task actually needed doing, he was always too busy, or waiting for the next commercial, or had his hands full, or something. Jane became tired of nagging and took out the garbage herself. The same thing happened with bill paying. Eric told her to throw the bills on his desk and he'd take care of them, but they were never paid until panic forced her to do it herself.

Finally she decided to stop mothering her husband. The next time the garbage needed to go out, she asked only once. After that, she started filling paper sacks beside the overflowing garbage can. The rest of the family made a fuss, but it took her husband five days of walking past the pile of refuse to notice it.

"I asked you to take that out the other day," Jane replied calmly. "I knew you'd get to it whenever you were able." She quietly communicated confidence in her husband, but also a line she would not cross.

Later, Jane took a similar action about the payment of their bills. Instead of bailing Eric out, she honored his commitment that he'd pay them. He didn't, of course, but after bill collectors began hounding him, he realized his wife was no longer going to mother him.

He said later, "I knew that all my life I just tried to get by. I didn't think of myself as lazy, but I suppose I was. I know I wasn't God's prize husband. Jane deserved better. But that day it hit me: things weren't going to get any better if I didn't change."

What Jane had been trying to accomplish for twelve years, the bill collectors and garbage odors took care of in three months![1]

Because the Powerful woman is so capable, it's tempting for her to do everything herself. However, in the long run, that's not a wise decision. She needs to get her man's input and allow him to shoulder his share of the responsibilities in their relationship. If she learns to consult with him, then uses her considerable energy and talent to implement their joint decisions on the home front, they can make a good marriage combination.

Powerful Woman + Perfect Man

The Powerful woman runs through life at breakneck speed, leaping obstacles in a single bound and conquering all opposition with her quick wit and sharp tongue. She thrives on action and is energized by spending time with people (especially when she gets to boss everybody around!). Unfortunately, this runs counter to a Perfect man's desire to stop and smell the roses, to enjoy the finer things of life.

The Powerful woman is a big-picture person who doesn't want to get bogged down with details like "How's this gonna work out?" She's running with the vision and doesn't want anyone to slow her down. Meanwhile, the Perfect man lives for details and is determined to slow her down at any cost.

If you want harmony in your relationship, have enough humility to admit that although you have great instincts, you're not infallible. Demonstrate respect for your honey by sitting quietly, listening to his careful analysis of the situation. It may very well be that his keen mind has honed in on a vital detail missing from your grand plan. Be thankful that he's willing to invest time preparing checklists and charts, and have enough sense to put them to good use.

Also remember that there are very few projects on this earth that need to be tackled right now. More often than not, haste makes waste. Be thankful that a detail-oriented man is encouraging you to do something you wouldn't otherwise do: take time to carefully think things through before springing into action.

When she marries, the Powerful woman often has a tendency to run roughshod over her husband's feelings. (Don't be fooled by all those marriage seminars that insist it's always the husband hurting the wife's feelings; in your marriage, it's far more likely that you'll be the one hurting his feelings.) A husband with a Perfect personality needs someone to listen to his innermost thoughts. Your tendency will be to brush him aside, advising him to "buck up" and "take it like a man." Nothing could be more detrimental to your relationship. Practice genuine listening, and actively resist the temptation to offer him solutions. He doesn't want solutions; he wants empathy and compassion.

Powerful Woman + Powerful Man

Wow, what a relationship. They'll either conquer the world or kill each other! When these two Powerful types get married, you can bank on major turf wars. They will continually clash over control, which both of them want and neither wants to concede. The key for this couple's survival is to closely define territorial lines of authority. The Powerful wife must recognize that her husband is the lord of her household, whether she likes it or not. But they'll be happier together if Tarzan realizes that Jane needs a portion of the jungle to rule, too. Maybe in the area of her career, a home business of her own or the chairmanship of a charity, or perhaps a small country to run. Whatever it is, she needs a place where she can exercise her natural urge to take charge in a positive, productive way. A healthy dose of mutual respect will go a long way toward keeping this marriage strong.

Also focus on the incredible potential you have together. I've met Powerful couples in joint ministry who accomplished unparalleled feats for God. More precisely, they allowed God to work *through them* to accomplish much.

Powerful Woman + Peaceful Man

When I was gathering stories for this book, I sent an email to several friends. Here's one response:

> I printed out your email and walked into the kitchen where my husband and I began to predict each other's Personality type. We discovered that I am Powerful, and he is Peaceful. I asked him what he thought you meant by "lord it over your husband," and he said it had to do with bossing him around all the time. I thought about that for about two seconds, then exclaimed, "I do *not* boss you around! You just need a lot of reminding!" He just looked at me and smiled, then we both burst into laughter.

Yes, the Powerful woman feels she is helping her man by providing him with twenty-four-hours-a-day, seven-days-a-week reminders. She's not. She's nagging him. And like the Perfect woman, she can drive her man away if she's not careful.

When a Powerful woman marries, she often steamrolls her agenda over her husband and the rest of the family. She's going to do what she wants to do, and if anyone has an alternative plan, she doesn't want to hear about it. If her Peaceful husband, in a sudden wave of resolve, puts his foot down and pursues *his* agenda for the family, she'll do everything in her power to make life miserable. And she's pretty good at it!

The Powerful woman's tendency to act now and think later gets the family into one difficulty after another, and her take-charge attitude often causes a scene in public. One woman joked, "I used to do this constantly—as in *daily*—and my husband would just die inside. The great news is: at this point, I only cause a scene every few weeks. So there is hope!" Since the Peaceful husband wants to avoid conflict at all costs, he becomes extremely upset over these incidents.

One of our former neighbors (actually, a sweet Christian lady) had gotten into so many fights with local store owners that her family was embarrassed to shop for everything from clothes to groceries. On one occasion, she got so intense "standing up for what was right" she was actually banned from shopping at that establishment. Her low-key, Peaceful husband suffered humiliation after humiliation. Eventually, resentment began creeping into the marriage. The Powerful wife could learn a thing or two from her Peaceful husband about how much further kindness gets you than anger.

A Powerful woman also tends to spend money without consulting her husband, which makes him angry, frustrated, and resentful. Sarah recounts an experience that stands out in her mind:

One time, I called an organization to ask if they would be willing to donate books for a charitable cause. Let me emphasize that: a donation. Somehow, I ended up purchasing sixty-five dollars worth of cookbooks. After I hung up the phone, I sat in shock, realizing what I had done. I knew my husband, who works so hard at putting together and following the family budget, was going to be furious. Worse than that, I knew how much it hurt him when I completely disregarded his carefully written-out budget proposals.

What on earth was Sarah to do? On this occasion, she reports that she actually handled it right.

I immediately started praying, "Lord, I don't want to dishonor my husband like this. I know he will be hurt and upset. Help!" A few hours later, the phone rang. The woman said my credit card number was written down incorrectly on the order form. I practically screamed, *"Great! Cancel the order!"* Well, that's not quite the reaction she was expecting. I'll bet she was completely baffled when she hung up the phone. But that night, there was peace in our household.

What if, instead, Sarah had chosen to be stubborn? What if she had said, "Oh, so what? Big deal. I did it, and I can do whatever I want. He'll just have to change his budget and make it work." An attitude like that will only serve to discourage your husband and hurt the cause of harmony in your home.

Florence Littauer describes a typical scenario in the Powerful-Peaceful marriage:

The [Peaceful] Personality doesn't like to be pushed, and yet when they are left on their own, they don't get around to doing what they promised to do. Dotty, a [Powerful] friend of mine who is trying to keep from running everything in the home, gave her [Peaceful] husband, Lewis, a major decision to make. In discussing vacation plans, he chose a certain resort on the coast. Lewis was to make the reservations. Each time Dotty asked if he had made them yet, he told her he would do it when he was ready, and she should stop nagging him. On the day they were leaving, Dotty summoned up a smile of hope and asked sweetly, "I assume you did make the reservations." His low-key comment was, "They always have cancellations." She was furious, and they drove in silence to San Diego.

When they asked the desk clerk about vacancies, he laughed at them. "You expect to walk into a beach resort in August and pick up a room? You must be kidding. There's not a space in town."

"That was insult enough," Dotty told me, "but then Lewis turned to me and said, 'You should have reminded me to call.' I lost my mind on that, burst into tears, and ran out to the car where I hit my fists on the fenders. I vowed I'd never count on him for anything again."

They finally found a room in an old motel next to an all-night diner. Lewis went promptly to sleep on the lumpy mattress, while Dotty lay awake livid all night.

In the morning Lewis said, "This may not be a luxury motel, but think of the money we saved."

Unfortunately, this scenario is typical of the merry-go-round the [Powerful] wife and [Peaceful] husband are on. He doesn't want to be pushed around and tells her so. She holds back, and then tries not to check on him. He neglects his responsibilities, and the ax falls. She gets upset and knows she can't trust him. She takes back control, and he tells everyone she picks on him. She comes across as the heavy and he looks like the typical henpecked husband.[2]

Here's a warning for Powerful women: when you marry, your husband is the most prone to burnout. If you keep lording it over him, you will crush his spirit, and your marriage will become a sad, empty shell. Sure, you'll get your own way, but you certainly won't get the man you married. You'll spend your life with only a shadow of the man he once was . . . and could have become.

Does it have to happen? Is a Powerful-Peaceful relationship doomed from the start? Certainly not. Yes, this is a tough Personality combination. It will become much easier when you finally admit to yourself that no matter how hard you try, you will never succeed in changing your man. Only God can do that! None of the self-improvement programs you develop for *his* self will do a drop of good. You can try it all: books, seminars, training programs, Bible studies, small groups, you name it. You can push and prod. But nine times out of ten, you'll find that the more you push, the more he will resist.

When you finally begin to understand the Personalities, when you finally accept him and begin trying to meet *his* emotional needs rather than trying to get him to meet yours, you will see remarkable progress in your marriage. There's so much you can learn from each other; don't settle for second best.

13

How the Peaceful Woman Smothers Her Honey

Peaceful Woman + Popular Man

If I were picking a girlfriend or wife, I'd pick a Peaceful woman. The truth is, she is by far the easiest Personality type to live with. However, she does have some faults, in particular her tendency to smother the ones she loves. Generally speaking, this is a very harmonious relationship, especially if the woman is content to play the background role while her man uses his personality to win friends and influence people. If he lands in a "people" position, like sales, he'll be able to bring home the bacon, and she will quietly, slowly fry it up in the pan. That slow business could be a problem for the fast-moving Popular guy, who may get annoyed that she can't keep up with his pace. In particular, he wants their house to be the center of the action: Super Bowl parties, company picnics, and the like. He wants to drag home a dozen basketball buddies and have her spring into action with refreshments. Since she doesn't do well with surprises—and she definitely doesn't do springing motions—he may get frustrated with her lack of spontaneity and enthusiasm. Since both the Popular husband and the Peaceful wife avoid work, their house will never be the neighborhood showcase. Then again, they probably won't care!

Warning to Peaceful women (I've had a warning for each of the Personality types, so even though you're sweet ladies, I'll issue one): once you marry, you tend to create selfish, dependent husbands who become a burden to you in your old age. And when you are gone, they are incapable of caring for themselves and become a burden to their family. What's more, they know they are a burden, and feelings of uselessness depress and overwhelm them. Stand by your man, sure, but don't let him stand on you. Let him stand on his own two feet or he may forget how.

Peaceful Woman + Perfect Man

These two may have conflict when they marry because the Perfect husband wants the perfect house, and the Peaceful wife just doesn't have the energy or initiative to create and maintain a spotless and flawlessly decorated home. As a rule, she avoids extra work whenever possible, whereas he thinks the extra mile is the starting point. If he wants to impress clients or cohorts with beautifully arranged dinner parties, he'd better be prepared to shell out money for a caterer. When his drive for perfection comes up against her brick wall of indifference, deafening silence can result.

This couple may also become completely isolated, because both are introverts and both can wield the silent treatment like a deadly weapon. This couple can live together in virtual silence for fifty years. Their marriage is dead, but they won't do anything about it.

I once stayed in the home of a Peaceful wife and Perfect husband. Within an hour of my arrival, I realized that this was *not* her idea. The husband, who was actually Perfect-Powerful, was the chairman of the elder board of the church at which I was conducting a weekend retreat. Without consulting his wife, he had volunteered her to play hostess for the weekend. I'm sure he assumed she would muster her energy and rise to the occasion. She didn't. He was a successful executive with a major corporation and had provided her with a huge mansion, which she had obviously neglected over the years. The guest room was run-down. There was nothing in the guest bath: no soap, no shampoo, no towels, nothing. When I awoke in the morning, there was nothing to eat, and the hostess slept right through the first session of the retreat. She showed up around lunch, looking like she'd just awakened.

Prior to my departure, he pulled me aside for a private conversation. (His wife had gone directly back to bed after the last session of the retreat.) We talked for some time, and I was deeply moved by his love for God and his concern for spiritual things. With tears in his eyes, he asked what to do about his wife. "She just doesn't seem to care about spiritual things. I had really hoped this weekend would give her the jump-start she needs. I try not to say anything, but I worry about her. All she does is sit in front of the television all day. She never wants to get involved at the church, never wants to learn anything new. She's a Christian, but she just doesn't seem to care."

I could sense his disappointment and encouraged him to pray for his wife. The truth is, unless she makes a decision to rouse herself from her slumber, the marriage will continue to be a deep disappointment to them both. But it doesn't have to be that way. My friend Terre and her husband have been happily married for years. She shares her secret:

We're both rather subdued, so there isn't a lot of open conflict in our marriage. There is *one* thing that really gets on my husband's nerves, though: little mistakes and accidents that just happen in the course of everyday life. The perfectionist in him just can't abide them because, as he says, these things wouldn't happen if people would just *think* about what they're doing. Corny as it sounds, he gets especially upset over spilled milk! If anybody spills milk, Steve literally jumps out of his chair trying to catch the upset glass. Then he turns on the offender and exhorts them to "*Think!* Just *think* about what your hands are doing!" I usually just sit there and say something consoling like, "Oops, there goes another one."

One day, after yet another spill, Steve sat down and moaned, "How many times do I have to go through this?" To which I muttered, "Until you get it right, I guess." Suddenly his perfectionist personality had a new angle to work on. These days, when somebody spills milk, he starts to jump, then forces himself to let it go. You can almost see the gears going around in his head thinking, "I must get this right!" After it finally registers with me that there is milk running all over the table and onto the floor, I'll get up and clean it. Order is restored. Peace reigns and life goes on. We're learning!

Peaceful Woman + Powerful Man

This is the way all couples are supposed to be, right? The man is clearly in charge as the head of the household. He goes off to corporate America and makes bundles of money. Or he launches his own wildly successful company and makes even more money. He thinks fast and looks sharp. She is content to stay in the background, quietly applauding his many achievements. She is perfectly content to submit to his every whim, because frankly, it's a whole lot easier than taking initiative herself. She goes along with whatever he plans, because it spares her from putting forth any effort.

Provided he's content to do all the work and she's content to hold on for the ride, this couple will enjoy the perfect marriage. But problems can develop if he wakes up one morning and thinks, *Wait a minute. I do all the work, all the thinking, everything. This woman is nothing but dead weight. She contributes nothing, accomplishes nothing. I might just as well toss her overboard.* And boom, she's gone without a second thought. On the other hand, she may get tired of him walking all over her and treating her like a piece of furniture. She may just rise up and demand a little R-E-S-P-E-C-T, which he is unlikely to give. He only respects accomplishments, and the Peaceful woman is not big on accomplishments. She may just walk out on him after twenty-five years of being pushed around, and if she does, she'll never look back.

To avoid either of those unfortunate scenarios, the Powerful husband needs to respect his wife for her people skills. It may be helpful for her to delicately point out that everyone likes her, and virtually no one likes him! And she, in turn, should try to demonstrate a little initiative from time to time, just to show her husband that she's still alive and kicking.

Peaceful Woman + Peaceful Man

Ah, picture Mr. and Mrs. Peaceful, sitting in their lazy old rocking chairs, watching life go by. The truth is, these two easygoing people will probably get along just beautifully when they marry: no confrontation, conflict, or crisis. So what's the problem? Well, there's not much excitement, either. They may just bore each other to death! They'll also have a tough time getting anything accomplished, so let's hope they inherit enough money to live on. If not, their financial woes will present an ongoing problem. They will have difficulty making decisions because neither one wants to impose his opinion on the other. But, hey, I know plenty of couples who wish they had such problems!

Possible areas of conflict may emerge because of their secondary Personality types. One partner will probably be Peaceful-Perfect while the other is Peaceful-Popular. In that scenario, the conflicts between the Perfect and Popular personalities will emerge. Fortunately, their overriding desire for peace should enable them to keep their cool.

A FINAL WORD

You did it! You made it all the way through this crash course on understanding the Personality types. By now you should have been transformed into the perfect girlfriend or wife. What's that? You're not perfect yet?

Well, I'm not perfect, either . . . and I teach this stuff!

Reading this material won't make you perfect, but studying it and applying what you learn will certainly make your life easier, while making you a little easier to live with. I would strongly urge you to go back and reread the portions of the book you highlighted. Jot down some notes about your Personality on a card and carry it with you wherever you go. When you've got a few extra minutes (waiting in line or sitting at the doctor's office, for example), pull out the card and prayerfully consider how you can implement these truths into your life.

At a minimum, I trust you've gained a greater understanding of why you act the way you do and how others perceive you. I hope you've begun building on your strengths and that you pray daily for power to overcome your weaknesses. I also trust that you have gained an increased appreciation for the man in your life and that you have developed some strategies to better meet his emotional needs.

Thanks for reading along with me. If this book has made a difference in your life or you have a hilarious or moving story you've just got to share, I'd love to hear from you.

Remember: God loves you and made you just the way you are!

Blessings,
Donna Partow
www.donnapartow.com

Appendix

Personality Test Word Definitions[1]

Strengths

1. *Adventurous*—willing to take on new and daring enterprises with a determination to master them

   Adaptable—easily fits in and is comfortable in any situation

   Animated—full of life; lively use of hand and arm gestures and facial expression

   Analytical—likes to examine the parts for their logical and proper relationships

2. *Persistent*—sees one project through to its completion before starting another

   Playful—full of fun and good humor

   Persuasive—convinces through logic and fact rather than charm or power

   Peaceful—seems undisturbed and tranquil; retreats from any form of strife

3. *Submissive*—easily accepts another's point of view or desire with little need to assert her own opinion

   Self-sacrificing—willingly gives up personal being for the sake of, or to meet the needs of, others

   Sociable—sees being with others as an opportunity to be cute and entertaining rather than as a challenge or business opportunity

   Strong-willed—determined to have his own way

4. *Considerate*—having regard for the needs and feelings of others

   Controlled—rarely displays emotions

   Competitive—turns every situation, happening, or game into a contest and always plays to win

   Convincing—wins through the sheer charm of her Personality

5. *Refreshing*—renews and stimulates; makes others feel good

   Respectful—treats others with deference, honor, and esteem

   Reserved—self-restraint in expression of emotion or enthusiasm

   Resourceful—able to act quickly and effectively in virtually all situations

6. *Satisfied*—accepting of any circumstance or situation

   Sensitive—cares intensely about people and situations

   Self-reliant—full dependence on personal capabilities, judgment, and resources

   Spirited—full of life and excitement

7. *Planner*—prefers to work out a detailed arrangement for the accomplishment of project or goal, and prefers involvement with the planning stages and the finished project rather than the carrying out of the task

   Patient—unmoved by delay; remains calm and tolerant

   Positive—knows it will turn out right if he's in charge

Promoter—urges or compels others to go along, join, or invest on the basis of his personal charm

8. *Sure*—confident; rarely hesitates or waivers

Spontaneous—prefers all of life to be impulsive, unpremeditated, and unrestricted by plans

Scheduled—makes and lives according to a daily plan; dislikes her plan to be interrupted

Shy—quiet; doesn't easily initiate conversation

9. *Orderly*—methodical and systematic

Obliging—accommodating; quick to do a task another's way

Outspoken—speaks frankly and without reserve

Optimistic—sunny disposition; convinces himself and others that everything will turn out all right

10. *Friendly*—a responder rather than an initiator, seldom starts a conversation

Faithful—consistently reliable, steadfast, loyal, and devoted sometimes beyond reason

Funny—sparkling sense of humor that can turn virtually any story into a hilarious event

Forceful—a commanding Personality whom others would hesitate to take a stand against

11. *Daring*—willing to take risks; fearless; bold

Delightful—a person who is upbeat and fun to be with

Diplomatic—tactful, sensitive, and patient

Detailed—does everything in proper order with a clear memory of all the things that happened

12. *Cheerful*—consistently in good spirits; promotes happiness in others

Consistent—stays emotionally on an even keel, responding as one might expect

Cultured—interested in both intellectual and artistic pursuits, such as theater, symphony, ballet

Confident—self-assured and certain of personal ability and success

13. *Idealistic*—visualizes things in their perfect form; has a need to measure up to that standard himself

Independent—self-sufficient, self-supporting, self-confident; seems to have little need of help

Inoffensive—seldom unpleasant or objectionable in behavior or speech

Inspiring—encourages others to work, to join, or to be involved and makes the whole project fun

14. *Demonstrative*—openly expresses emotion, especially affection, and doesn't hesitate to touch others while speaking to them

Decisive—quick, conclusive, judgment-making ability

Dry humor—exhibits "dry wit," usually humorous one-liners that can be sarcastic in nature

Deep—intense and often introspective with a distaste for surface conversation and pursuits

15. *Mediator*—consistently reconciles differences in order to avoid conflict

Musical—participates in or has a deep appreciation for music; is committed to music as an art form rather than simply the fun of performance

Mover—driven by a need to be productive; is a leader whom others follow; finds it difficult to sit still

Mixes easily—loves a party and can't wait to meet everyone in the room; never meets a stranger

16. *Thoughtful*—considerate; remembers special occasions; quick to make a kind gesture

Tenacious—holds on firmly, stubbornly; won't let go until the goal is accomplished

Talker—constantly speaking; often telling funny stories and entertaining everyone around; feeling the need to fill the silence in order to make others comfortable

Tolerant—easily accepts the thoughts and ways of others without the need to disagree with or change them

17. *Listener*—willing to hear what others have to say

    Loyal—faithful to a person, ideal, or job, sometimes beyond reason

    Leader—a natural-born director; driven to be in charge; often finds it difficult to believe that anyone else can do the job as well

    Lively—full of life; vigorous; energetic

18. *Contented*—easily satisfied with what she has; rarely envious

    Chief—commands leadership and expects people to follow

    Chart maker—organizes life, tasks, and problem solving by making lists, forms, or graphs

    Cute—precious, adorable, center of attention

19. *Perfectionist*—laces high standards on himself and often on others, desiring that everything be in proper order at all times

    Pleasant—easygoing, easy to be around, easy to talk with

    Productive—must constantly be working or achieving, often finds it very difficult to rest

    Popular—life of the party and therefore much desired as a party guest

20. *Bouncy*—a bubbly, lively Personality; full of energy

    Bold—fearless; daring; forward; unafraid of risk

    Behaved—consistently desires to conduct herself within the realm of what she feels is proper

    Balanced—stable, middle-of-the-road Personality, not subject to sharp highs or lows

Weaknesses

21. *Brassy*—showy; flashy; comes on strong; too loud

    Bossy—commanding; domineering; sometimes overbearing in adult relationships

    Bashful—self-conscious; shrinks from getting attention

    Blank—a person who shows little facial expression or emotion

22. *Undisciplined*—lack of order permeates most every area of his life

    Unsympathetic—finds it difficult to relate to the problems or hurts of others

    Unenthusiastic—tends to not get excited, often feeling it won't work anyway

    Unforgiving—difficulty releasing or forgetting a hurt or injustice done, apt to hold on to a grudge

23. *Reluctant*—reserved; uncommunicative; especially when the situation is complex

    Resentful—often holds ill feelings as a result of real or imagined offenses

    Resistant—strives against or hesitates to accept any other way but her own

    Repetitious—retells stories and incidents to entertain you, not realizing he has already told the story several times; constantly needs something to say

24. *Fussy*—calling for great attention to trivial or petty details

    Fearful—often experiences feelings of deep concern, apprehension, or anxiousness

    Forgetful—lack of memory usually tied to a lack of discipline and not bothering to mentally record things that aren't fun

    Frank—straightforward; outspoken; doesn't mind telling you exactly what she thinks

25. *Impatient*—finds it difficult to endure irritation or wait for others

    Insecure—apprehensive or lacking confidence

    Indecisive—finds it difficult to make any decision at all (not the Personality that labors long over each decision in order to make the perfect one)

    Interrupts—a person who is more of a talker than a listener, who starts speaking without even realizing someone else is already speaking

26. *Unpopular*—intensity and demand for perfection can push others away

    Uninvolved—has no desire to listen or become interested in clubs, groups, activities, or other people's lives

    Unpredictable—may be ecstatic one moment and down the next, or willing to help but then disappears, or promises to come but forgets to show up

    Unaffectionate—finds it difficult to verbally or physically demonstrate tenderness openly

27. *Headstrong*—insists on having his own way

    Haphazard—no consistent way of doing things

    Hard to please—a person whose standards are set so high that it is difficult to ever satisfy her

    Hesitant—slow to get moving and hard to get involved

28. *Plain*—a middle-of-the-road Personality without highs or lows and showing little, if any, emotion

    Pessimistic—while hoping for the best, this person generally sees the downside of a situation first

    Proud—one with great self-esteem who sees himself as always right and the best person for the job

    Permissive—allows others (including children) to do as they please in order to keep from being disliked

29. *Angered easily*—a childish flash-in-the-pan temper that expresses itself in tantrum style that is over and forgotten almost instantly

   Aimless—not a goal-setter with little desire to be one

   Argumentative—incites arguments usually because she is certain she is right no matter what the situation may be

   Alienated—easily feels estranged from others often because of insecurity or fear that others don't really enjoy his company

30. *Naïve*—simple and childlike perspective, lacking sophistication or comprehension of what the deeper levels of life are really about

   Negative attitude—seldom positive and often able to see only the down or dark side of each situation

   Nervy—full of confidence, fortitude, and sheer guts, often in a negative sense

   Nonchalant—easygoing, unconcerned, indifferent

31. *Worrier*—consistently feels uncertain, troubled, or anxious

   Withdrawn—a person who pulls back to herself and needs a great deal of alone or isolation time

   Workaholic—an aggressive goal-setter who must be constantly productive and feels very guilty when resting; not driven by a need for perfection or completion but by a need for accomplishment and reward

   Wants credit—thrives on the credit or approval of others. As an entertainer, this person feeds on the applause, laughter, and/or acceptance of an audience

32. *Too sensitive*—overly introspective and easily offended when misunderstood

   Tactless—sometimes expresses himself in a somewhat offensive and inconsiderate way

   Timid—shrinks from difficult situations

Talkative—an entertaining, compulsive talker who finds it difficult to listen

33. *Doubtful*—characterized by uncertainty and lack of confidence that it will ever work out

   Disorganized—lack of ability to ever get life in order

   Domineering—compulsively takes control of situations and/or people, usually telling others what to do

   Depressed—a person who feels down much of the time

34. *Inconsistent*—erratic, contradictory, with actions and emotions not based on logic

   Introvert—a person whose thoughts and interests are directed inward, lives within herself

   Intolerant—appears unable to withstand or accept another's attitudes, point of view, or way of doing things

   Indifferent—a person to whom most things don't matter one way or the other

35. *Messy*—a state of disorder and disorganization

   Moody—doesn't get very high emotionally, but easily slips into low lows, often when feeling unappreciated

   Mumbles—will talk quietly under his breath when pushed, doesn't bother to speak clearly

   Manipulative—influences or manages shrewdly or deviously for her own advantage; will get her way somehow

36. *Slow*—doesn't often act or think quickly, too much of a bother

   Stubborn—determined to exert his own will; not easily persuaded; obstinate

   Show-off—needs to be the center of attention; wants to be watched

   Skeptical—disbelieving; questions the motive behind the words

211

37. *Loner*—requires a lot of private time; tends to avoid other people

    Lords over others—doesn't hesitate to let others know she is right or in control

    Lazy—evaluates work or activity in terms of how much energy it will take

    Loud—laugh or voice can be heard above others in the room

38. *Sluggish*—slow to get started, needs push to be motivated

    Suspicious—tends to suspect or distrust others or ideas

    Short-tempered—has a demanding, impatience-based anger and a short fuse; anger is expressed when others are not moving fast enough or have not completed what they have been asked to do

    Scatterbrained—lacks the power of concentration or attention; flighty

39. *Revengeful*—holds a grudge and punishes the offender, often by subtly withholding friendship or affection

    Restless—likes constant new activity because it isn't fun to do the same things all the time

    Reluctant—resistant or unwilling to get involved

    Rash—acts hastily without thinking things through, generally because of impatience

40. *Compromising*—will often relax his position, even when right, to avoid conflict

    Critical—constantly evaluating and making judgments, frequently thinking or expressing negative reactions

    Crafty—shrewd; can always find a way to get to the desired end

    Changeable—has a childish, short attention span; needs a lot of change and variety to keep from getting bored

NOTES

Chapter 1

1. Created by Fred Littauer. Personality Profile from *Personality Plus* by Florence Littauer, copyright 1992 by Florence Littauer, used by permission of Florence Littauer and Revell Books. NOT TO BE REPRODUCED. Copies may be ordered by calling CLASServices, (800) 433-6633, or visit *www.thepersonalities.com*.

Chapter 4

1. Ruth Tucker, *From Jerusalem to Irian Jaya* (Grand Rapids: Zondervan, 1983), 257.
2. Ibid., 259.
3. Oswald Chambers, *My Utmost for His Highest* (Uhrichsville, OH: Barbour, 1991), 218.
4. Florence Littauer, *Personality Plus* (Grand Rapids: Revell, 1992), 126.
5. Andrew Murray, *Humility* (Minneapolis: Bethany House, 2001), 53.

Chapter 5

1. Littauer, *Personality Plus*, 130.
2. Stephen Ministries, 2045 Innerbelt Business Center Drive, St. Louis, MO, 63114. (314) 428-2600.
3. *Current* catalog, (800) 848-2848, or visit www.currentcatalog.com.

Chapter 6

1. Florence Littauer and Marita Littauer, *Personality Puzzle* (Grand Rapids: Revell, 1992), 201.

Chapter 7

1. According to Tim LaHaye in *The Spirit-Controlled Temperament* (Wheaton: Tyndale, 1993).

2. Tim LaHaye, *Transformed Temperaments* (Wheaton: Tyndale, 1993), 163.

3. Littauer and Littauer, *Personality Puzzle*, 202.

Chapter 8

1. Littauer and Littauer, *Personality Puzzle*, 203.

2. Ibid.

Chapter 9

1. LaHaye, *Transformed Temperaments*, 191.

2. Tim LaHaye, *Understanding the Male Temperament* (Grand Rapids: Revell, 2001), 87.

3. Mark Harris, Don Koch, and Stephanie Lewis, "The Measure of a Man," (Cool Springs, TN: Paragon Music Corp.), 1996.

Chapter 12

1. Annie Chapman, *Smart Women Keep It Simple* (Minneapolis: Bethany House, 1992), 30–31.

2. Littauer, *Personality Plus*, 159–60.

Appendix

1. Created by Fred Littauer. Personality Profile from *Personality Plus* by Florence Littauer, copyright 1992 by Florence Littauer, used by permission of Florence Littauer and Revell Books. NOT TO BE REPRODUCED. Copies may be ordered by calling CLASServices, (800) 433-6633, or visit *www.thepersonalities.com*.

Donna Partow is an author and motivational speaker on a mission to empower people to maximize their lives. She has traveled and worked throughout the United States and on six continents, including such diverse countries as Egypt, Turkey, Colombia, Thailand, and Papua New Guinea. She's as comfortable teaching in a mud church in Mozambique as she is speaking to thousands at a leadership conference.

Donna has been featured on hundreds of radio and television shows. Her books have sold a million copies worldwide and have been translated into numerous languages. Some of her bestselling titles include *This Isn't the Life I Signed Up For . . . But I'm Finding Hope and Healing* and *Becoming the Woman I Want to Be: A 90-Day Journey to Renewing Spirit, Soul & Body*.

Donna is a social media pioneer and offers a broad range of internet-based classes. Learn more at www.donnapartow.com.

"If you're stuck in a rut in your personal
Bible study . . . or you long for God to use you
in fresh new ways . . . or you and your small group
are tired of pat answers . . . this book is for you!"

—SUSAN ALEXANDER YATES, author of
A House Full of Friends and *And Then I Had Kids*

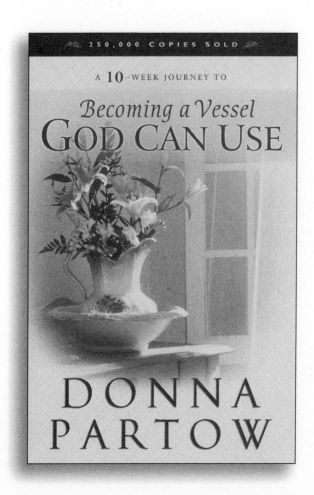

a division of Baker Publishing Group
www.BethanyHouse.com

Available wherever books are sold.

You *can* become the woman God wants you to be. Let this powerful guide renew your energy and determination.

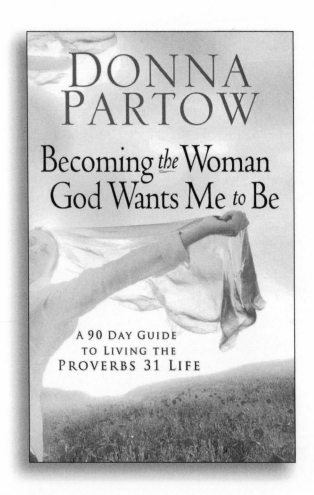

"Donna's plan will renew you from the inside out— spirit, soul, and body!"

—Danna Demetre, author of *Scale Down*

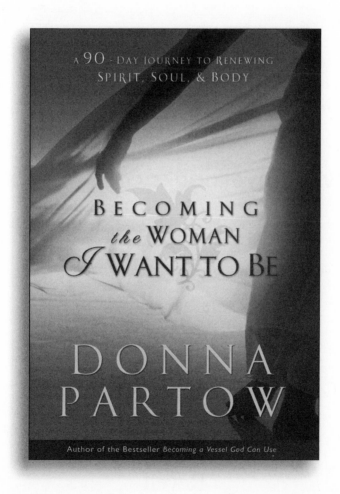